NO MORE POINTLESS MEETINGS

NO MORE POINTLESS MEETINGS

Breakthrough Sessions That Will Revolutionize the Way You Work

MARTIN MURPHY

AMACOM

American Management Association

New York • Atlanta • Brussels • Chicago • Mexico City • San Francisco
Shanghai • Tokyo • Toronto • Washington, D.C.

Bulk discounts available. For details visit:
www.amacombooks.org/go/specialsales
Or contact special sales:
Phone: 800-250-5308
Email: specialsls@amanet.org
View all the AMACOM titles at: www.amacombooks.org

This publication is designed to provide accurate and authoritative information in regard to the subject matter covered. It is sold with the understanding that the publisher is not engaged in rendering legal, accounting, or other professional service. If legal advice or other expert assistance is required, the services of a competent professional person should be sought.

Library of Congress Cataloging-in-Publication Data
Murphy, Martin, 1942–
  No more pointless meetings : breakthrough sessions that will revolutionize the way you work / Martin Murphy.
    p.   cm.
  Includes index.
  ISBN 978-0-8144-3168-9 (pbk.) — ISBN 0-8144-3168-2 (pbk.)
  1. Business meetings.   2. Organizational effectiveness.   I. Title.
  HF5734.5.M87 2013
  658.4'56—dc23   2012025180

About AMA
American Management Association (www.amanet.org) is a world leader in talent development, advancing the skills of individuals to drive business success. Our mission is to support the goals of individuals and organizations through a complete range of products and services, including classroom and virtual seminars, webcasts, webinars, podcasts, conferences, corporate and government solutions, business books, and research. AMA's approach to improving performance combines experiential learning—learning through doing—with opportunities for ongoing professional growth at every step of one's career journey.

Printing number

10 9 8 7 6 5 4 3 2 1

for Linda Clare

CONTENTS

CONTENTS

An Operational Tool
Organizational Learning
A Strategic Mindset
Zen and the Workflow Planner
Effective Decision Making
A Final Thought

Chapter 6

CONTENTS

Chapter 1

WHY MEETINGS FAIL:
REFRAMING WORKFLOW MANAGEMENT

This book will convince you that in the digital age, conventional meetings are obsolete, and when compared to advances in other areas of organizational management, the current art of human collaboration seems archaic. It needn't be.

I can walk into any conference room cold, without any prior knowledge of the organization or the meeting that is about to begin, and lead it in a manner that gets more done in a shorter period of time than anyone in the room has ever experienced. The get-together can be with the board of directors, top executives, departmental managers, supervisors, team leaders, or any mix of people and disciplines; it doesn't matter: I get superior results every time I facilitate a collaborative event—because I don't use meetings for collaboration.

At its most elemental, this book is intended to provide managers and supervisors who currently conduct meetings with a transformative alternative they can use immediately to get more done in less time. In addition, it provides them with workflow management tools to access and leverage the cognitive and creative capabilities of the individuals who report to them in a manner that creates value for employees, consumers, and stakeholders.

Meetings have survived as the primary collaborative process because it is assumed that an individual, once promoted to a leadership position, already knows how to effectively leverage human capital. The facts don't support this—all of us still get trapped in meetings that squander time we'll never recover. While the number and complexity of issues that require resolution accelerates, unsatisfactory meeting outcomes are still an everyday event. Before we get into detailed instruction for the workflow management protocols you're about to be introduced to, it will help to take a look at how we currently collaborate within organizations.

For most executives, managers, and supervisors, the meeting is the only work management tool they've ever used for collaboration. The drill is ingrained: Everyone gathers in a conference room, and the most senior executive both conducts *and* participates in the meeting at the same time. This wasteful collaborative ritual takes place millions of times daily in organizations around the globe. And, while its shortcomings are acknowledged, it has been the principal means for collaboration over the course of many generations.

Granted, we now have distance conferencing capabilities, but digital conferencing platforms are basically delivery vehicles—their ultimate effectiveness as a collaborative tool is dependent upon users having the ability to leverage the intellectual and creative potential of the individuals participating in the dialogue.

If managers are doing a poor job of collaborating in person-to-person gatherings—and be assured that they are—digital collaborative performance will be even less effective. Right now, this reality is overshadowed by excitement over the diversity of impressive delivery vehicles and platforms for distance conferencing. That excitement will prove hollow unless we also upgrade the human element of the collaborative equation.

GUIDING PRINCIPLES

Reframing workflow management activities into four broad categories of need transforms the effectiveness of workflow management in general and collaboration in particular. Those categories—the need to manage issues, to solve problems, to innovate, and to plan—yielded the following collaborative elements of a workflow management system (see Figure 1.1):

1. The Issues Management Session
2. The Innovation Session
3. The Problem-Solving Session
4. Ongoing Planning

The fourth element, Ongoing Planning, provides the means to capitalize on exponential change by building speed-to-market capabilities.

In the next four chapters, we'll explore processes for

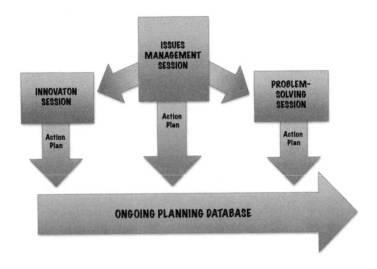

Figure 1.1   Workflow management system.

conducting Issues Management, Innovation, and Problem-Solving sessions and introduce an Ongoing Planning structure. There are, however, two principles on which all of these sessions are based:

1. Content and process must be kept separate.
2. The boss (or the highest-ranking person in the room) should not run workflow management sessions.

Separate Content and Process

While there's little doubt about the need to upgrade the quality of workplace collaboration, how to do so can be a challenge. I'm going to tell you how to get it done quickly and in a manner that's least disruptive to everyday workflow management. We'll begin with the core elements of all interpersonal communications: content and process. Content refers to *what's* being discussed, the subject or purpose for having a meeting in the first place.

Process refers to virtually everything else, for instance:

- How loudly are people speaking?
- Who's talking the most?
- Who's apparently not listening?
- Who's not participating?
- How many are in the meeting?
- Who are they?
- How long is the meeting scheduled to run?
- How's the energy level in the room?
- Is there a spirit of openness and teamwork?
- Is the overall tone of the meeting positive?
- Is the boss present?
- Are things getting accomplished?

Most collaboration problems occur in the arena of process, not content. This happens because most managers focus on content and ignore process. While content and process are equally important, few managers understand the importance of separating them or possess the ability to do so.

As already mentioned, conventional meetings are characterized by the ranking manager both *running* the session and *participating* in content discussions. This is the main reason meetings are not as productive as they could be: You simply cannot do a decent job of facilitating a meeting and participate in the content of the meeting at the same time. Facilitating a meeting is a full-time job.

The workflow management sessions you'll learn about here provide the means to leverage the collective intellectual and creative potential of a group. The sessions are customized to meet different collaboration needs and, when conducted properly, yield outcomes that are dramatically superior to typical meeting results. All workflow management sessions have a facilitator who fulfills this role. This facilitator orchestrates the session in a manner that enables the group to get more done in a shorter amount of time than in a regular meeting.

Collaboration is transformed by the simple act of keeping content and process separate. Facilitators don't participate in content discussions. Their job is to handle process only and to do so in a manner that motivates all participants to contribute to the maximum of their ability. At the beginning of every workflow management session the facilitator needs to get three agreements from the group:

1. The facilitator accepts responsibility for meeting process.
2. The group accepts responsibility for meeting content.
3. Both the facilitator and the group commit to an outstanding workflow session outcome.

Facilitators don't run workflow sessions without these agreements. This is not as dramatic a statement as you might think. During the past three decades I've run hundreds of workflow management sessions, and I've never had a group refuse to grant me control of and responsibility for process. Nevertheless, agreement about this is a very important part of the workflow management process. It establishes the importance of recognizing and separating the two dynamics—content and process—with just a dash of drama.

With a new group, a facilitator can expect to be tested a few times on the promise to stay out of content, and as facilitators adjust to the process, they can expect to be tempted sometimes to give their opinions about particular content issues. Just remember that the facilitator's job is to handle process only, and a facilitator who succumbs to discussing *any* content issue, no matter how trivial, undermines the group's trust and triggers all the woes of traditional meetings.

As the facilitator of a workflow session, you're responsible for coordinating a diversity of personalities and agendas. To say that this requires full-time concentration is an understatement. However, when participants realize that you're not going to take part in any content discussions, they'll trust you with the welfare of the session and participate with enthusiasm.

Why the Boss Shouldn't Run Meetings

The most senior person in attendance definitely should *not* run a work session. As a matter of fact, if there's more than one person in the room who knows how to facilitate, the task should go to the most junior. This frees up the greatest number of senior personnel to contribute to content.

If there's any doubt in your mind about the logic of this practice, consider the fact that it's easier to acquire the skills needed to run a productive workflow session than it is to accumulate the knowledge, experience, and wisdom brought to a session by the CEO or other senior managers.

When the most senior executive in the room runs a meeting, an array of counterproductive interpersonal dynamics is triggered that impedes optimum collaboration. While politicking and fear-based reticence rank high on that list, the single biggest reason meetings fail is that the individual running the session isn't familiar with the collaboration practices we're discussing.

A Facilitator creates a level playing field, where input from everyone is encouraged and given the same consideration. Thus, a normally domineering boss is neutralized and prevented from unintentionally intimidating lesser souls so that they don't contribute.

The fundamental purpose of meetings is to utilize the collective human capital of a group to get things accomplished. When that opportunity is properly presented, good things happen and even the most timid are motivated to contribute; the energy in the room sparkles; radical ideas and breakthrough solutions (which in a normal meeting wouldn't see the light of day) are solicited and suggested without fear of judgment.

As your comfort level with the workflow management process grows, you'll be able to explain the absurdity of mixing content and process with examples that strike a chord.

You've been in meetings where everyone is talking at the same time and no one is listening to what others are saying because they're busy rehearsing what they're going to say. Since everyone in the room is actively engaged in content discussions and no one is minding the store (process), outcomes from these get-togethers don't reflect the true potential of the assembled talent.

Routinely, a much deeper reserve of intellectual and creative potential remains untapped, good content goes unrecognized, and follow-up is sporadic, all because process went untended. This doesn't happen in the workflow sessions you'll be introduced to here.

THE ISSUES MANAGEMENT SESSION

The goal in this session is to surface all of the issues that need to be addressed, in both the short and the long term. The Issues Management Session is the session you'll first consider when previewing a workload. In some cases, issues can be resolved in-session with an Action Plan that indicates who's responsible and a due date. For example, if customer confusion regarding the corporate website is an issue, the Action Plan might indicate an assignment for the social media manager to update or redesign the platform with an agreed-upon delivery date.

Some issues, however, cannot be resolved in an Issues Management Session, and in that case the issue would be addressed in one of two follow-up sessions: an Innovation Session or a Problem-Solving Session. (Remember that there is always an Action Plan, even if the action indicated is simply to promote an issue to an Innovation or Problem-Solving Session.)

THE INNOVATION SESSION

If the issue requires an innovative new concept or new thinking or a new direction, the Action Plan for that issue should be to schedule an Innovation Session. In product development, often the most exciting sessions are the Innovation workflow management sessions, which normally result in hundreds of new ideas that are generated in a short period of time. In Innovation workflow management sessions, the imagination is unfettered and there are no boundaries or barriers to creativity. Eventually, of course, the session identifies and culls the strongest of these ideas and promotes them to Action Plan status.

THE PROBLEM-SOLVING SESSION

The unresolved issues from the Issues Management Session might be defined as problems, in which case they need to be moved to a Problem-Solving Session. The difference between the definition of an *issue* and the definition of a *problem* is often blurred, as many people use these words interchangeably. There is, however, a clear distinction. All problems are issues, but not all issues are problems.

For example, an astute manager might see the opportunity to upgrade systems and procedures in anticipation of an influx of new business. This is an issue, not a problem. However, if she waited until the new business volume reached the point of stressing individuals because of antiquated systems and procedures, *that* would be a problem.

ONGOING PLANNING

Each of the three sessions just described ends with an Action Plan, which is submitted to (1) the people who participated in the work session and (2) the Ongoing Planning Database.

The database is vital, since it not only accumulates the fodder for Ongoing Planning but is essential for ensuring that all managers operate from a unified strategic perspective—a consequence of being up to date with the workflow management activities of all other managers. This is discussed in Chapter 5, "The Ongoing Planning Process."

ENTRY POINTS

Three dynamics—Entry Points, Leverage, and Questions—play a key role in upgrading the quality of thought that drives intellectual performance in general and Problem-Solving in particular. These interrelated tools enable a dramatic upgrade of the cognitive capabilities of managers and supervisors.

The starting points, or Entry Points, are created by the questions we ask to better understand the precise nature of the issue being addressed or the problem to be solved. How often have you experienced the frustration of being unable to resolve a problem and then discovered you've been addressing the wrong problem or going down the wrong path? This is usually the result of choosing a weak Entry Point in the Problem-Solving process. (See Figure 1.2.)

Most managers operate from the perspective of what they *do* know as the Entry Point to solve problems and resolve issues. This is actually the converse of effective Problem-Solving. As you'll see, the Problem-Solving Session

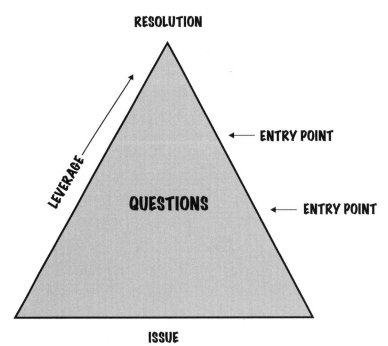

Figure 1.2 Elements of the Problem-Solving process.

begins with an exploration of what we *don't* know rather than a reiteration of what we *do* know. Once there's agreement about the definition of the problem, you'll be able to guide the group to identify the best *Entry Point* for tackling the problem. The selection of a strong Entry Point is the most crucial step in the Problem-Solving and issue resolution process.

The concept of *Leverage* is intimately related to Entry Points. Every Question that's asked about a problem has a leverageability quotient. The more highly leveraged a Question, the more quickly it leads you to the solution.

When we finally ask the *right* Question, we have the solution to the problem, or at least we'll be pointed in the right direction. If we get a partial solution, we continue to apply the Question Exercise to the part of the solution we don't yet have.

You'll find that Questions have a significant effect on a group's ability to solve problems—that the quality of the Questions brought to what's *not* known shortens the Problem-Solving and issue resolution process. Moreover, you'll find that a healthy dissatisfaction with the quality of a group's initial Questions gets them closer to the key Question, which in turn, indicates the most productive Entry Point.

MANAGING YOURSELF

Keep in mind that whenever we have the courage to go outside our comfort zone to learn something new, we traverse a confidence curve. So don't be surprised if your anxiety level goes up a notch or two when you run the first Issues Management Session.

For example, when you make a mistake or forget where you are in a highly productive, everything's-happening-at-once session, just ask the group for help. I enjoy losing my way every now and then, especially when I'm experimenting with a new Innovation or Problem-Solving technique. I have no qualms about turning to the group and saying, "I'm lost; somebody help me out here." There is nothing that bonds the members of a group and their leader faster than displaying courage by telling the truth. The group will remind you exactly where you went astray, and together you and the group will regain alignment.

Not only is the resultant bonding enjoyable for both you and the group, but productivity will go through the roof. Once you've experienced this, your ability to lead others by example will mature and you'll undergo a personal transformation in your understanding of the collaborative process; you'll empower others to go beyond their comfort zones to get more accomplished faster. Strive for a relationship of this kind every time you conduct a session with your team.

STRUCTURE OF THIS BOOK

Chapters 2 through 5 explain and illustrate in detail the reframed elements of workflow management—three collaborative sessions and the Ongoing Planning Database.

Although the collaborative sessions are kept separate for the purposes of this book, in reality you'll find that the different sessions are interconnected. A Problem-Solving Session, for example, often indicates the need for an Innovation Session that could be run immediately or scheduled for later. Figure 1.3 illustrates the full potential of the interactions among the four protocols.

While the workflow management sessions described here involve groups, they are not limited to team utilization; the session structure can be adapted for one-on-one use, involving only two people, or for solo workflow management purposes. Chapters 6 and 7 explain the process for conducting one-on-one and solo sessions.

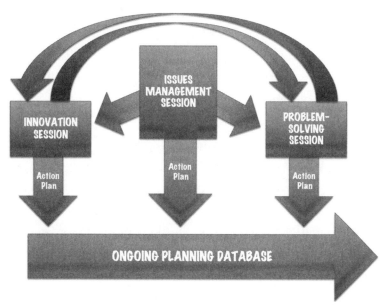

Figure 1.3   Workflow session interactions.

Chapter 8 provides Innovation and Problem-Solving coaching to ensure that workflow management capabilities are constantly improving, as well as ideas, tips, and suggestions for how to ensure this; ready-to-use ideation exercises; and instruction on providing an unlimited supply of Ideation jump-start exercises by creating them yourself.

I recommend that you learn the group workflow management sessions in the sequence in which they are presented—Issues Management, Innovation, and Problem-Solving—and become comfortable with them before you use the one-on-ones or solo versions. The logic of this learning sequence is simple: Each group session introduces exercises and processes that require familiarity with the session's predecessor. There's a similar interdependency with regard to the one-on-ones and solo versions; it's best to learn the former before the latter.

The Issues Management Session is the easiest to learn, and it is the workflow management tool you'll end up using in the place of everyday meetings. By starting all collaborative events with an Issues Management Session, you'll get more done in a shorter period of time, with consensus regarding Next Steps and their ownership.

The Innovation Session is the most exciting because it provides access to the imaginative and creative talents of the individuals who report to you. Since innovation and speed to market are core strategic skills required for success in a rapidly evolving global economy, the benefits of mastering the process of the Innovation Session and the tools and exercises within it are self-evident.

Problem-Solving Sessions produce transformative results because they use the creativity and innovation tools from the Innovation Session. Familiarity with the Innovation process makes Problem-Solving more effective and an easier skill to master.

Ongoing Planning depends on the three collaborative sessions being in place before it can be triggered. For that reason, it is presented as a fourth workflow management element after the three collaborative sessions.

Chapter 2

THE ISSUES MANAGEMENT SESSION

A s we'll use the term, an *issue* is anything that occurs, that should have occurred, or that you wish would occur that has relevance to your job or area of responsibility. Issues comprise the dynamics one is responsible for managing. This includes anything related to the welfare of the organization that requires attention, something that needs to be resolved, a trend to explore, an opportunity that could be exploited, or a problem that needs to be solved. An issue might be relevant only to one's job or it might be something bigger that affects the entire organization, the competition, or the industry in general.

Issues have differing degrees of importance: The most important are classified as *Critical Issues* and require immediate attention or resolution. The timely assessment of all issues minimizes the numbers that become critical.

The Issues Management Session is the most versatile of the workflow sessions we'll introduce. It can be considered the default session for most collaboration needs, since it enables you to comfortably handle expanding workloads and streamline day-to-day workflow management.

The Issues Management Session enables managers and their teams to get more done in a shorter amount of time; a thirty-minute session typically outperforms a two-hour conventional meeting. An upgrade from traditional meetings, it transforms workflow skill levels and enables managers to dramatically improve the productivity of those reporting to them. In addition to expediting the resolution of workflow management issues, the session streamlines communications between divisions, departments, business units, and individuals. Systems and procedures are routinely upgraded when the session is utilized, and individuals are more willing to take early ownership of issues. Any issues that can't be resolved in-session are earmarked for one of the two other collaboration sessions, Innovation or Problem-Solving.

A good practice is to begin all team gatherings with an Issues Management Session, especially if there are many items that need timely resolution or if you have any doubt about which workflow session to use.

The rest of this chapter explains the step-by-step process for conducting an Issues Management Session, illustrated through an ongoing case study (details have been changed to ensure client confidentiality).

SESSION LOGISTICS

You can conduct a session with as many as twenty people. I've found a ten- to twelve-person session is best. Experiment with groups of various sizes, and discover your own comfort level. As

---

you'll see, an Issues Management Session can also be conducted alone or with just one or two others. It's a flexible workflow tool and a powerful management skill to possess.

Workflow sessions can be scheduled for as little as twenty minutes or for several hours, depending on the amount and complexity of issues to be addressed and the time available. Obviously, longer sessions must include breaks. I've found it helpful to have a ten-minute break every hour. Also, let the group know that it's okay to leave the session at any time, and request that it be done as unobtrusively as possible. Request that cell phones be set to vibrate and that all calls be taken outside of the conference room.

All group workflow sessions have the same setup requirements: three easels with large paper pads (self-adhesive are best), colored markers for the facilitator, and writing pads and pens for participants.

The Innovation and the Problem-Solving sessions require three additional easels, one on each side and one on the rear wall of the conference room, for team breakouts. Seating is flexible: A conference table big enough to seat all participants will suffice. In its absence, chairs can be arranged to suit the Facilitator. If possible, especially for all-day Innovation and Problem-Solving sessions, opt for a conference room with windows for some natural lighting and plenty of room for breakouts.

THE CASE STUDY

As with many assignments, this one had an intriguing twist. A well-established company was losing share of market to a competitor that had been acquired by a large multinational. The acquiring company was investing heavily in new product development and was also growing through acquisitions. This meant it could develop new products on a larger scale, and that capability was now available to my client's major competitor.

The client organization was family owned, a pioneer in the product category, and determined to prosper without being acquired. My assignment was to help the company identify the means to remain a highly profitable, privately owned enterprise.

I'd had contact with only one person at the client organization, the vice president of marketing, who'd retained me on the basis of a referral from a client in an unrelated industry. I'd spoken to her on the telephone, got an overview of the situation, and arranged a full-day work session with her and a group of senior executives, including the CEO. It was agreed that a second day, or a portion thereof, might be needed, and everyone's calendar was kept open to accommodate that possibility.

We'd agreed for the meeting to be in their boardroom, which could comfortably accommodate the fifteen participants and had plenty of room for breakout sessions. The gathering included individuals responsible for the major divisions, departments, business units, and disciplines, and encompassed manufacturing, marketing, research and development, sales, human resources, administration, and so on. Three easels had been provided and placed at the front of the room for my use; three others were placed at the rear and on each side of the large conference room. Electronic displays were available but not needed for what I had in mind.

The Issues Management Session

Step One: Laying the Groundwork

The most important step in any workflow management session is how well one explains the difference between conventional meetings and workflow management sessions and the concepts of content and process. Begin the session by spending as much time as you need for participants to be clear about these differences, as discussed in Chapter 1. Emphasize the fact that you will not get involved in content discussions but will focus on process exclusively. This change in procedure is one of the key differences between meetings and workflow management sessions. Once participants understand the difference between content and process, ask for an agreement with them regarding your respective roles.

Information Gaps

Once you have clearly established an agreement on the different roles, write the heading "Information Gaps" on one of the easels. In any collaborative work session there are many questions that emerge during the process. In some cases, the questions are answered during the session; in other cases, these Information Gaps have to be filled after the session. Explain to the participants that you will record all the unanswered questions that pop up during the session.

Managers with the wisdom to embrace the unknown have a competitive edge: They define themselves as part of change, not apart from it. They appreciate why the timely resolution of missing information is one of the core values that differentiates top-tier organizations from their competitors. Consequently, these men and women are difficult to catch by surprise; more likely, they catch the competition by surprise.

In an information-driven global economy, the advantages of having processes and tools in place to resolve Information Gaps as they are uncovered help build a team's knowledge, awareness, and creativity. You need to seed that mindset at every opportunity.

Unanswered Information Gaps should not be allowed to accumulate. They are included for resolution in the Action Plan that is developed as the last step in any workflow management session.

Some individuals are puzzled by the importance I assign to Information Gaps until they're reminded of a particular digital age fact: Most organizations operate in knowledge-driven, information-saturated industries where change is occurring at exponential speed. At any given point, the scope of what is not known is greater than what *is* known, and that gap is widening faster than our ability to stay current. Thus, a proactive attitude toward Information Gaps is critical for successful workflow management. Anything less suggests management-by-hope.

Step Two: Identify the Purpose of the Session

Once you have the groundwork laid and the logistics in place, the next step is to define the purpose of the session. Don't launch into a session unless all participants have a clear understanding of the purpose of the session. For this session I wrote on one of the easels: "As a consequence of being acquired by a multinational company with deep pockets, our major competitor now has the wherewithal to outspend us significantly in business development efforts of all types. What can we do to protect share of market for our product line?" Everyone agreed that this statement captured the purpose of the meeting.

Step Three: Surface All the Issues

Once you have an agreement on the purpose, the next step is to surface all of the possible issues related to the purpose of the session. Instruct the participants to write "Issues" on their personal writing pads and, without discussion, write down all of the issues they think must be addressed. Give participants the following instructions to ensure the most comprehensive list of issues possible:

> Without discussion, please write down as many issues as possible that you think we should address in this session. Start with issues that fall within your area of responsibility and then expand your list without restriction.
>
> Feel free to expand your perspective to include issues that are normally outside your area of responsibility. Please write quickly and be prepared to read portions of your list aloud so that the issues can be displayed.
>
> At this point of the session the emphasis is on quantity of issues, so you don't need to give what you write a lot of thought; just write as many issues as you wish as quickly as you can.

In the session with my clients, I gave the participants a short time limit (five minutes) for this and then went around the room and took just two issues from each person at a time. I recorded each issue on one of my easels and had a volunteer mount the sheets on the conference room walls.

As I expected, there were many issues from the first round. That's normal—people come into most work sessions (or meetings) with lots of preconceived ideas, and it's important to get these out of their heads and onto paper as soon as possible before the real work can begin. Without this step, people tend to stay attached to their preconceptions and are not as open to dissenting viewpoints as they could be.

The issues from the opening rounds ranged from department-specific to industrywide. Examples included the following:

- How does this impact our marketing budget?
- What are the PR implications?
- Can we continue going head-to-head with a competitor that all of a sudden has very deep pockets?
- Will that competitor price us out of the category?
- Should we reposition our brand or product line?

MAKE SURE THEY UNDERSTAND

When I'm running a workflow management session, I always ask if there is anyone who does not understand an instruction before I tell them to start. If I don't ask, there are likely to be interruptions midcycle by participants who are uncertain or confused, and that can ruin the pace of the session.

Step Four: Narrow the List to *Critical* Issues

Once you have a list of issues, you must help participants identify the Critical Issues on the list. Define the term *critical* in general terms because what's critical to one person may be inconsequential to another. For example, say, "Let's agree that a Critical Issue is one that you feel is important enough to warrant group discussion or at least group awareness."

Ask participants to identify the five issues they think are the most critical, and give them five minutes to do so. Then go around the room taking no more than two critical issues from any one person at a time, and display them (in a small group, I'd take only one at a time). Usually, there is some overlap, which you can handle by adding a check mark to an issue that has already been submitted. Remember that all of this is done without discussion.

You now have a list of the most critical individual issues. By the end of this round, we had dozens of critical issues. Here are some examples:

- What perception does our target audience have of us?

- What business are we really in?

- Since we're the pioneer in this product category, is there a difference in the nature of brand loyalty to us vs. our competitor?

- If most of the parent company's business units outsource to offshore manufacturing sources, will it do this with our competitor's domestic manufacturing operation?

NOT EVERY ISSUE IS CRITICAL

When you ask participants of a work session to narrow the issues to the most critical, some laugh and say that all the issues are critical. It certainly may seem that way at first, but as they are forced to make choices, participants start to see that not every issue is actually critical.

Step Five: List the Top Ten Critical Issues

The next step is to further refine and focus your list of Critical Issues, eventually getting a consensus on the top ten issues. Before you do that, however, ask whether any participants have issues they consider critical but that not might be recognized as such by anyone else.

Some people are easily intimidated by a group setting. Some work alone and outside of any team setting. Yet their input is potentially just as important as anyone else's. For that reason, I'm always willing to go the extra step and coax from these particpants what might turn out to be very serious issues if not addressed in a timely manner. I make it clear to the group that if any individual considers a particular issue to be critical, it gets onto the final list of Critical Issues. In the same vein, when an individual is uncertain about a particular issue being critical, I always treat it as critical.

Once you have compiled your list of Critical Issues, break the group into teams and ask them to come up with their top ten Critical Issues, within five minutes.

For example, I asked the client participants to break out into three teams with as much cross-pollination as possible—I asked them to team up with people they don't work with every day. The teams converged around the three easels designated for that purpose. Each team selected a scribe to do the recording, and that role rotated every few minutes.

I allotted them fifteen minutes to come to a group agreement about which issues and solutions should be in the final ten. I encouraged discussion and urged them to walk around and review the issues posted on the walls. Since it was their first opportunity to mingle and talk freely, this was a high-energy point in the session. I went from group to group to clarify the instruction as needed.

At the end of the fifteen minutes, I asked them to reconvene at the front of the room with their top ten lists. Participants were free to sit or stand for this. All sheets were mounted, and a team representative from each group read the group's list and explained the reason for their selections. We now had three lists composed of varying issues, many of them solution-oriented.

Group A's list included the following issues:

- In our advertising and marketing, could we link the acquired company (competitor) in terms of its parent company's global size and outsourcing operations to create a David vs. Goliath context and capitalize on the domestic vs. offshore manufacturing (American made, by Americans, etc.)?
- Let's go offshore with our own manufacturing.

Group B's list included the following issue:

- Let's change advertising agencies from our current regional shop to one with a significant new product develop-

29

ment client roster, nationally and internationally; this will leverage our in-house product development capabilities, at little additional cost.

Group C's list included the following issues:

- Can we improve our own new product development capability by upgrading our in-house systems and procedures?
- Let's take advantage of our smaller size and outperform them through innovative customer service.
- Let's expand the product category to include innovative new products that we can introduce at a preemptive pace.

This third group also suggested developing the following:

- A generic line of category products, priced below the branded products on the market, including our own; the line would be introduced with innovative trade promotion initiatives and not deplete national advertising budgets.

Now is the time to get a consensus on the Critical Issues. Address the group as follows:

I'm going to point to each issue, and I'd like you to rank it in terms of its importance. Give it a score of three if you think it needs to be resolved immediately, a score of two if it needs to be resolved soon, and a score of one if it can wait to be resolved until the threes and twos are handled.

Then point to issue number one and get a ranking of importance from everyone in the group. Accord each issue a number of check marks corresponding to each person's score for that particular issue (a score of 3 gets three checks, etc.).

At the end of this step, each issue has a line of check marks beside it. Count the number of check marks for each issue and record each total with a colored marker. You now have a ranking, which establishes the sequence we'll use in addressing these issues. The issue with the highest number of check marks is first to be addressed.

At this point, confirm that no issue has been omitted because of oversight or social discomfort. To prevent that from happening, ask the group, "Does anyone have an issue they consider critical that is not displayed? If so, please give it to me and I'll board it now."

Step Six: Resolve the Issues or Move Them to Another Session

Some of the Critical Issues on the list can be resolved in-session. Others are more complicated and require that actions be taken out of session. Some defy any kind of resolution in the Issues Management Session and require a Problem-Solving or Innovation Session. Your goal is to help the group identify which of the issues can be resolved in-session and provide the Next Steps for those issues that can't.

On one of your easels, write "Action Plan," point to the first issue, and ask the group:

Can Critical Issue number one be resolved right now?
Take three minutes to decide, as a group. Please start.

Allow group discussion for about three minutes. Your goal is to quickly determine whether Critical Issue #1 can be resolved without a Problem-Solving or Innovation Session. Be careful when you're at this stage in an Issues Management Session—it's easy to lose your process focus and get involved in the discussion.

The objective is to facilitate group discussion about the resolution of Critical Issue #1. If the group seems to be making headway, let them run with it and stay out of the way. If after about three minutes they seem to be stymied, however, intervene with a process suggestion: to schedule the issue for resolution via a Problem-Solving or Innovation Session and then direct the group to the resolution of Critical Issue #2.

For our purposes, let's assume the group thinks that Critical Issue #1 does not require Problem-Solving or Innovation and they want to take care of it right now. Maybe it's an issue that simply needs the coordinated input of a few people to avoid becoming a more serious problem.

In any case, since a formalized Problem-Solving or Innovation Session is not required, get resolution on Critical Issue #1 as quickly as possible and promote it to Action Plan status. By *resolution,* I mean that the group agrees on what the Next Steps should be, they have identified who's responsible for making this happen, and they have established a deadline. This could be a one-step process or a series of tasks that requires the attention of several people. The important point is that resolution of Critical Issue #1 has begun and the Next Steps have been identified and agreed upon. Metaphorically speaking, the ball has been moved forward.

You've now completed one cycle of a simplified Issues Management Session. To continue, select Critical Issue #2, resolve it if possible, and advance it to Action Plan status.

With my client group, we addressed one Critical Issue at a time to determine whether that issue, or part of it, could be resolved right then and there. Some issues were resolved quickly. These included a decision to "update target audience segmentation trends, brand loyalty statistics, and outdated consumer research within and adjacent to the product category."

In addition, many Information Gaps had been identified in-session. They included "Questions about the acquiring company—their outsourcing strategies and procedures; the history of acquisitions they executed within the last ten years, including their respective performance pre- and post-acquisition, etc." Responsibilities for getting answers to these questions were assigned, with due dates.

Issues that could not be resolved in-session were scheduled to be addressed in one of two other workflow management sessions, either Problem-Solving or Innovation. In view of the nature and time sensitivity of the issues on the table, the decision to resolve these the following day was unanimous.

Step Seven: Write the Action Plan

All workflow sessions conclude with an Action Plan. Action Plans serve as the means to record the conclusions that were drawn, the solutions that were identified, and the agreements that were made in any work session. An important function of Action Plans is that they ensure outcomes are implemented in a manner that optimizes accountability, transparency, and speed-to-market performance. In the session involving my client, for example, every issue that was identified was noted in the Action Plan, which also described whether the issue was resolved in the session (and if so, how—for example, were tasks assigned related to the issue?) or whether the issue was moved to the agenda of a future Problem-Solving or Innovation Session.

Specifically, an Action Plan consists of four vertical columns labeled "Tasks/Next Steps," "Responsibility," "Due Date," and "Report."

Tasks/Next Steps

An issue is promoted to Action Plan status when agreement is reached about Next Steps. This does not necessarily mean that the issue has been resolved or the problem solved. It could be an issue the group was unable to resolve in-session (in a timely manner), so they decided to address it in a subsequent Problem-Solving Session. This column covers the nature of any issue's disposition, so it should be wide enough to accommodate descriptions of related tasks and spin-off activities.

Responsibility

When all of the steps to resolve a particular issue have been identified, I ask for volunteers to take responsibility for completing the tasks. An alternative is for the ranking executive in attendance to assign them. The names of the individuals who have been assigned particular responsibilities are recorded in the "Responsibility" column. Often, the nature of a task requires coordinating with others and may involve several steps. It's important to be clear about who is responsible for each step.

Due Date

The commitment to complete the task by the agreed-upon date is a critical aspect of the Action Plan. With a group new to the process, this is a good time for you to emphasize the importance of due dates and deadlines. In addition to taking responsibility for completing tasks, these individuals also agree to inform the group if the task or project looks like it will take longer to complete than initially expected. This is important because of the interconnectivity of all tasks and projects. It also fosters a spirit of cooperation, teamwork, and ownership—critical considerations for organizations that are committed to best-of-class collaboration.

You'll find it best to delay entering any dates in the "Due Date" column until all other aspects of the Action Plan have been completed. This gives individuals who have volunteered to complete more than one assignment the opportunity to review the full list of their commitments and agree to realistic delivery dates.

Report

This column identifies the individual(s) to whom task results will be submitted. As a general rule, it's good practice to inform all participants of all task outcomes. However, there may be circumstances when the "Report" column includes an individual who did not attend the meeting—perhaps a particular executive whose authorization is required to move things forward.

It's also important that Action Plans be submitted to the Planning Database within minutes of their completion so they can be assessed for strategic relevance, timelines can be coordinated with related projects, and fresh interconnectivities with other issues and activities in the organization can be assessed. This is addressed in Chapter 5, "The Ongoing Planning Process."

DON'T FORGET THE INFORMATION GAPS

Don't forget to include the Information Gaps in the Action Plan. They should all be treated as Critical Issues and warrant the same attention. I keep a group in the Issues Management mode until all of the Critical Issues have been addressed and promoted to Action Plan status. Then, time permitting, I'll switch sessions to handle the unresolved issues with a Problem-Solving or Innovation Session. If we run out of time or folks are tired, we simply schedule the appropriate follow-up session(s).

Chapter 3

THE INNOVATION SESSION

Imagination is more important
than knowledge.
—ALBERT EINSTEIN

The Innovation Session is the work management session to use when you want to tap into the creative potential of a group. It's the most exciting of the workflow management sessions—a unique combination of creativity and instant gratification.

The session is more structured than brainstorming, and outcomes are superior in terms of both quality of ideas and quantity. (I'm presenting it as the second of the three collaborative sessions because it introduces the reader to core creative thinking skills and exercises that play an important role in the third collaborative session, Problem-Solving.) The Innovation Session has many applications, and use of it is indicated when any of the following needs are identified:

- Development of new products or services

- Upgrade of systems and procedures

- Streamlining of intradepartmental communications

- Identification of alternative marketing strategies

- Development of a name for a new product, service, or initiative

- Identification of a unique promotional idea or initiative

- Jump-start of a stalled Problem-Solving Session

An Innovation Session comprises four phases: Ideation, Building, Evaluation, and Action Plan.

Ideation: The goal of the first phase of the Innovation Session is to enable and encourage the participants to generate as many ideas as possible. A key for success in this phase is to suspend any self-editing on the part of the participants.

Building: In the second phase of the Innovation Session, participants take their ideas and partial ideas and turn them into more defined and detailed concepts.

Evaluation: The third phase of the session is for evaluating the concepts and determining the most likely to succeed. Next Steps are then established for moving the new product idea from concept to the next stage in product development.

Action Plan: All ideas, concepts, and Next Steps are captured for the Ongoing Planning Database.

A key ingredient for success in an Innovation Session is to ensure that the Ideation and Building phases are kept separate from the Evaluation phase. This is because Ideation and Building are creative activities while Evaluation is cognitive—based on rational and practical thinking. If you mix them, the rational dynamic (Evaluation) dominates, and you end up with next to nothing in terms of new ideas. This is a common occurrence in brainstorming sessions.

It may help you to keep in mind that people are always willing to tell you why an idea won't work (often without being asked); we're surrounded by experts on why things won't work. It's a subconscious default mode for most people, and you must be ready to handle it quickly when it comes up during the Ideation or Building phase of a session. Be assured it will happen, especially with newcomers to the process and at the beginning of a session, while people are adjusting to the procedure.

When people start evaluating, just remind them what they're doing and ask them to stop. Another way of handling this situation is to ask the group to self-regulate by gently reminding each other not to evaluate. For many, it's a tough habit to break. Just be insistent, and everyone will get the message eventually.

SESSION LOGISTICS

An Innovation Session can be scheduled for an hour, a few hours, or a full day. Interestingly, when people complete an Innovation

---

Session of any length, they appear to have more energy than when they started.

As a general rule of thumb, if the goal is to develop new product ideas, try to allocate as much time as possible for the project. This will allow adequate time for Ideation, Building, Evaluation, and the Action Plan. It will also ensure you'll generate hundreds of new product ideas, many of which will be worthy of qualitative and quantitative testing.

For those not familiar with consumer research, a focus group is an example of qualitative testing, and it's not statistically projectable. Quantitative testing, on the other hand, includes enough people to be statistically predictive within a few percentage points. Political polls conducted via telephone with a large number of respondents are an example of quantitative testing.

In the consumer goods industry, qualitative testing is used to determine whether a new product idea is worthy of being promoted to the more expensive quantitative testing stage. It can also be used to design any subsequent quantitative testing.

When possible, conduct Innovation Sessions in the flesh as opposed to virtually. The reason for this is that the success of the Innovation Session is very much a consequence of the facilitator's ability to connect with and motivate the individuals in the room on many levels. Eye contact, body language, standing vs. sitting, seat changing, voice inflection, and dozens of different exercises and processes are an integral part of the session. Ideation, group breakouts, colors, and sounds are all tools the skillful facilitator knows how and when to use. At the very least, conduct an in-person session before you use distance conferencing technology for the task.

An Innovation Session can be productive with as many as twenty participants. However, if input from a larger number of individuals is desired, you'd be better off scheduling two or more smaller sessions. While I prefer working with a ten- to fifteen-person group, you may be more comfortable working with fewer people—especially in the beginning, when you're becoming familiar with the process. Experiment with groups of different sizes, and discover what works best for you. After a few sessions, the size of a group won't be an issue for you.

THE CASE STUDY

As with the Issues Management Session, we'll use a case study based on an actual company to illustrate the steps in the Innovation Session. (Again, the details have been changed for client confidentiality.) The company in this case study makes several leading candy brands. The goal of the session was to develop new product ideas for the growing "healthy snack" product category.

Fifteen managers with varying levels of seniority and responsibility from different divisions, departments, and disciplines within the company were in attendance. The departments and functions represented in the session were marketing, new business development, research and development, brand management, advertising agency personnel, sales, promotions, and several other decision makers. (We'll return to the details of the case study shortly.)

The Innovation Session

Getting Started

As with any workflow management session, begin an Innovation Session by clearly explaining to participants the difference between a conventional meeting and a workflow management session; then clarify the difference between content and process.

When you conduct any workflow management session with individuals who are new to the process, you need to establish an explicit agreement with them on the roles of the participants and that of the facilitator.

Information Gaps

During the session, make sure that participants know they are encouraged to raise questions for group consideration at will. Request a volunteer to handle the task of writing unanswered questions on the Information Gaps sheets and mounting them on the walls of the conference room.

A word of caution: It's easy to forget about Information Gaps when so many other things are happening in an Innovation Session. A good way to prevent this is to thank the person who volunteered each time he or she gets up to record an unanswered question. In addition to being good manners, this draws attention to the value *you* place on embracing what's not known. Put some effort into helping newcomers appreciate the importance of Information Gaps, and don't be tempted to rush this aspect of the session setup.

ABOUT BREAKS

Let the group know what you have in mind with regard to session length and breaks. If you are in the middle of a particularly productive exercise or task, you or the group may not want to stop for a break. When that happens, simply get their okay to continue with the session until a more appropriate time to break.

After a break, ask each participant to sit in a different seat. This is an important part of the Innovation Session because it requires participants to change comfort zones, increases their attention levels, and adds to the overall energy level in the room. It also serves as a means of overcoming another hurdle of complacency.

PACE

Speed plays an important role in workflow management sessions because it engages individuals and neutralizes many interpersonal distractions. Most people aren't used to collaboration where structure is imposed for purposes of maximizing outcomes.

Be very conscious of this in an Innovation setting, especially during changeup from one phase or exercise to another; transitions need to be fluid and seamlessly executed. The pace of a productive session should not be interrupted. Once people embrace the process and get in the "zone," you want them to stay there for as long as possible. Lengthy transitions dampen a group's enthusiasm, and the magic of the moment is lost.

Clarify Session Purpose

The first thing to do is to make sure there is agreement on the purpose of the session. To avoid spending too much time on this, write what you understand the goal to be on one of the easels.

Purposefully state the goal as broadly as possible, and then ask the group if they agree with your interpretation. Without making it a drawn-out affair, allow them to guide you in rewording the statement if necessary. In the session for the candy manufacturer, the objective was clear-cut: "to generate viable new product ideas for the 'healthy snack' market category." I displayed it at the front of the room.

Phase One: Ideation

You are now ready to lead the group in the *Ideation* phase, the first of the four phases of the Innovation Session.

In a roomful of people about to tackle the task of creating new product ideas, be assured that most of them already have some new product ideas or partial ideas in their heads. As in the Issues Management Session, you need to get those ideas out of their heads and onto paper as quickly as possible.

Write "Ideas" on an easel and instruct the group as follows:

Our goal is to generate new product ideas. Most of you have some ideas already, and we want to capture all of those before we continue. With that in mind, and *without* discussion, would you please write as many new product ideas as you can. Please strive for quantity of ideas. Absurdity is encouraged. Do not attempt to evaluate—that's the easy part, and we'll do it later. For now, let your imagination run wild. Emphasize the outlandish, the improbable, and the impossible, as opposed to the logical or feasible. Forget viability for the moment and strive for quantity of ideas. You have three minutes to do this. Does anybody not understand the instruction? Please start.

Note that the combination of short completion cycles (three minutes) and the instruction "without discussion" increases the energy level in the room. It short-circuits cognitive comfort zones and encourages energized participation. In addition, it invokes the agreement you made a few moments before: You're in control of the process, you know what you're doing, and we're in this together. You'll find that most groups appreciate this structure and leadership. Those few who don't are converted once they start seeing the results.

For all of the same reasons, let a group know when it has thirty seconds left to complete tasks and exercises.

THE LEADERSHIP ATTITUDE

A high positive energy level is a key component for successful Innovation. If you can make sure people enjoy themselves while

---

adhering to process structure, you'll have a productive session. In that regard, you have to lead by example, so don't bring any personal negativity to the session; show the group that you enjoy your role, which is to assist a roomful of mainly pragmatic minds to switch mental gears and tap into their creative capabilities. For some of them, this will be a new experience.

Your attitude should reflect confidence, warmth, empathy, and an ego-free control of the room. Much of that can be conveyed without words. One key to a successful Innovation Session is to let the group see that you're enjoying yourself. Be upbeat, validating, courteous, and inspiring.

Also, keep in mind that the words I use to communicate instructions fit my personality and delivery style. You should use your own style of delivery to get the same points across. Just get a clear understanding of what needs to be communicated from this reference and make the session work for you, on your terms. As you become familiar with the process, you'll see opportunities to customize and improvise to fit specific needs.

Remember, you're about to orchestrate a creative process that requires individuals to go outside of their respective comfort zones—more so than in any of the other collaboration sessions we'll discuss. Many individuals are reluctant to do that in front of their colleagues, so they need to trust that you know what you're doing and they're not going to be embarrassed or made to look foolish.

Displaying

At the end of the first three-minute period, instruct the group to stop writing. Go around the room and ask each participant to read aloud one or two of their ideas. At this point the ideas are usually conservative compared to later suggestions.

These are a couple of the ideas that emerged from the candy manufacturer participants:

- A line of protein snacks for high school athletes during half-time
- V8-type popsicles of different veggies and fruits for younger kids

Don't take more than two issues at a time—especially with a large group. The reason for taking only two ideas from each person is that many people have similar ideas and by the time you get to them they complain that all of their ideas have already been boarded. For the same reason, change the order in which you accept ideas for boarding in every round.

Display all the ideas on an easel. Continue until everyone's ideas are displayed. Write fast: You don't want to be the one slowing things down. In addition, keep a conversation going with the person whose issues you're displaying because when you're writing, your back is partially turned to the group. Since you've lost eye contact with them, substitute voice contact. (This is an example of attention to process—a detail that differentiates workflow management sessions from normal meetings. Once I get things going, I usually ask for a volunteer to take over the task of mounting the sheets on the walls.)

ALWAYS CLARIFY

Whenever you're writing someone's idea on an easel, don't be afraid to ask for clarification or to double-check that you're getting it right. I always confirm that the authors of these ideas agree that I've displayed them accurately. This is an important measure because every idea that's offered comes from an owner who has a relationship to the idea that must be acknowledged if I want that person to continue contributing to the session.

So if Jane, for example, has an idea for a potato chip with a unique commingling of sweet and savory flavors, I make sure that I understand exactly what she has in mind, and I stay with her until I capture this idea to her satisfaction.

The converse is also true, however. I can't spend too much time with Jane's idea, or the session will get bogged down. As your comfort level improves, you'll be able to capture the essence of ideas with very few words; you'll develop your own shorthand style and amaze people at the speed with which you can capture an idea and display it to the satisfaction of its author.

I also say thank you to each person for every idea they share. This courtesy helps to set the tone for an upbeat, enjoyable, and productive session.

With a standard session group of fifteen participants, you typically get approximately seventy-five ideas from this step. They might range from completely new ideas for products or services that are not on the market to those that exist but can be improved upon through better packaging or repositioning for a different market subsegment, for example.

Note that new product development isn't restricted to "new" products that don't exist—thus, we use the term *business development*. All new product introductions fall under the umbrella of business development; business development, however, is not restricted to new product introductions. Acquisitions, for example, are a common business development strategy and may not involve any new product development.

Ask for More Ideas

By now the group is a bit more relaxed with the process, and their imaginations have been stirred by the ideas of their colleagues. To capitalize on this, ask participants to take another three minutes to use the ideas displayed on the walls to trigger additional new product ideas.

While the group is working, urge participants to relax and feel free to write "half-ideas" as well as batty ideas. A half-idea is an incomplete idea and it can be more valuable than a complete idea. Here's why: In a roomful of minds sharing a common purpose, a group synergy develops. Think in terms of the whole being greater than the sum of its parts. Usually a breakthrough idea is a combination of the partial ideas, batty ideas, inklings, and hunches of more than one person.

Batty ideas are as valuable as partial ideas. A batty idea is so ridiculous it makes us laugh. For example: "a snack that regenerates itself within twenty-four hours if you put the empty wrapper in a sealed sandwich bag" or "warm candy."

Encourage half-ideas and batty ones to capitalize on the collective creative potential in the room. Partial ideas and batty ideas take seed in the collective mind and are usually harvested in the *Building* phase of the Innovation Session, which comes later.

This is a good time to introduce some of the creativity exercises—such as the Genie Exercise, which uses the image of a genie granting five wishes—that are described in the next section and at the end of the chapter (see also Chapter 8). These exercises are intended to spark new and unexpected ideas by helping participants to tap their imaginative capabilities with enthusiasm.

Any More Ideas?

When the time is up for the second round of Ideation, go around the group taking just one or two ideas from each person and board them. The participants in the candy manufacturer's Innovation Session produced ideas such as these:

- A candy that's in between dessert and candy, like mini-desserts
- A candy that's a fruit in disguise
- A candy that's mostly air

Now you have a decision to make: Do you go for a third round of Ideation or switch gears? This is a judgment call based on your feel for what's left in the group's creative tank. You don't want to wear out the participants, and you don't want them to get bored by repeating a nonproductive task.

You might conclude that the participants still have some unexpressed ideas. If so, initiate a third round and display everyone's contribution by taking just one idea at a time from each person. Also, reverse the order in which you accept the ideas from participants.

If the group seems to be bursting at the seams with ideas, do a fourth round of Ideation. Basically, repeat Ideation cycles until it appears the group is completely out of ideas.

MAKE 'EM LAUGH

During the Ideation phase, continue to stoke a sense of positive urgency in the room by constantly walking around, and never miss an opportunity to validate and make people laugh. Laughter is an important ingredient in the Innovation process. It helps release the creative juices. (By the way, if you don't think you're funny enough to make people laugh, just poke gentle fun at some of your own mannerisms as you facilitate the Innovation Session. We're all funny when we take ourselves too seriously.)

Creativity Exercises That Spark the Imagination

Most people are ruled by a "cognitive" mindset, which means that they always tend to be logical and rational. When you are trying to develop extraordinary, unexpected, and groundbreaking ideas, such as a new product that takes the market by storm, a cognitive mindset is more of a hindrance than a help. Your job as a facilitator is to help participants break free of their rational and logical selves, and this book provides exercises to accomplish that.

Escaping the cognitive mindset and tapping into the imagination is important to the success of the workflow management sessions, especially the Innovation Session. I use a wide variety of exercises to accomplish this. What follows is an example of how this process works. (Additional exercises can be found in Chapter 8.)

Genie Exercise

The Genie Exercise is an imagination-stretching exercise. Ask the participants to use a clean sheet of paper, and then give them the following instruction:

> You've just found the proverbial lamp with a genie inside. You're alone. The genie appears and tells you that you have five wishes; you must decide on your list of wishes within the next five minutes. You must request five wishes, not four or six. And you may *not* wish for an unlimited number of wishes. Does anyone not understand the instructions? You have three minutes to complete this. Please start.

Let the participants know when they're within thirty seconds of the time limit. When the time is up, ask the group to quickly form into three teams as equal in size as possible. With the candy manufacturing group, I opted for three teams of five persons each. Make sure the teams are as diverse in their makeup as is feasible, and caution against people teaming with the same individuals they work with every day. Encourage as much cross-pollination as possible in terms of rank, discipline, departments, and so forth.

It's important to spend as little time as necessary going from individual to team exercises in order to take advantage of the high energy level of the group. With practice, you'll be able to orchestrate changes in a group's composition with speed and fluidity.

Provide each group with a large pad on an easel and some colored markers. To the extent possible, locate the teams to ensure some degree of privacy. If your conference room isn't large enough for this, you may be able to arrange for the breakout sessions to utilize adjacent office space.

Once the teams are formed, instruct team members to share their wish lists with their group. They do this orally; there is no need for any writing. Give them five minutes for this.

When the time is up, ask each participant to write down three new product ideas, on their writing pads, not their easels. For the candy manufacturer group, this meant three new product ideas for *any* category of snacks, in addition to the "healthy snack" category.

Once the team members have written down three new product ideas, tell them:

> The genie has changed his mind about how he wants you to handle the wishes. Instead of individual wishes, he wants each team to come to an agreement on a list of five team wishes. So there will be no individual wishes granted unless it's one of the five team wishes.
>
> Select one team member to be the scribe for the group. That person's job is to help the group agree on the five team wishes and write them on the large pad. The scribe can swap roles with any other person on the team after five minutes. You have ten minutes. Please start.

Let the group know when they have thirty seconds left, and then challenge each team member to write at least three additional new product ideas. When the time is up, take just one new product idea from each team member and board it.

You've just given the group two exercises that could keep them busy for the next several hours. Instead, they were given a few minutes for the exercises. This provides another window through which to access creativity.

Now reconvene the teams as a group. Ask a scribe from each team to mount the team wish list at the front of the room, and give the group a minute or two to review these and ask for clarification where necessary. Then give the group the following directive:

> Using as stimuli the team wish lists displayed here, write
> at least three new product ideas on your personal pads.

At this point, challenge the group to reach consensus on a group wish list. Obviously, participants will need to converse, but remind them that time continues to be a factor. Give them five minutes to agree on a group wish list. You'll function as their scribe and assist the group as needed. This group wish list will be used to spark a whole new set of ideas.

BREAKS

Keep an eye on the clock to ensure that groups get a ten-minute break every hour. A hardworking group might choose to delay a break for a few minutes because they don't want to interrupt a highly productive Ideation exercise. This is fine, as long as you've made it clear that anyone can leave the room at any time.

In addition, keep track of how much time is left for the other phases of the session. As a general rule, I dedicate the morning to Ideation and Building, and the afternoon to Evaluation and the Action Plan.

Although time is important, it's also important not to just depend on the clock to schedule breaks. A good facilitator remains aware of the group's energy level. Don't run the participants ragged. Stay tuned in, and let them know you are concerned for their comfort and energy levels. Frequently ask them how they feel and whether they'd like a break. Acknowledge their hard work; validate their output and commitment to the session.

Mind-Reading Exercise

The Mind-Reading Exercise is a powerful drill to help participants stretch their imaginations. Ask them to consider—without talking—the consequences of everyone on the planet having the ability to read the minds of everyone else. Challenge them to impose no boundaries on the scope of their imaginations. They are to simply list some of the consequences of everyone being able to read other people's minds. Allow five minutes for this exercise.

Let the group know when they have one minute left for this exercise, and then again when they have thirty seconds to finish. Take only one response from each participant. Don't display them. Just ask for volunteer participants to read aloud one entry from their list.

As with every creativity exercise, the goal here is to distract participants' "logic only spoken here" guardian and access their imaginations, if only for a few valuable moments. As entertaining as it could be, spend as little time as possible on the fantasy aspect of this exercise and focus on the opening it creates to access the group's individual and collective imaginations.

Once the volunteers have read a few of the imagined mind-reading consequences aloud, ask the group to write as many new product ideas or partial ideas as they can in the next three minutes—again without talking. Encourage them to go for quantity and absurdity. Remind them not to evaluate or self-censor. The sky's the limit here; it's their opportunity to get paid for being nuts.

Let the group know when they have thirty seconds to go. At the end of three minutes, stop them and ask for volunteers to display their new ideas. Ideally, everyone in the group will share their ideas; however, never put someone on the spot to do this. No one likes that kind of pressure, and it may cause some people to shut down.

Recognizing when to stop and change gears is a judgment call. As a rule of thumb, I keep going as long as the group is being productive and having fun. When they stop having fun, the group takes a ten-minute break.

What-If Exercise

This is one of the creativity exercises I used in the Innovation Session with the candy manufacturer group. Give the group the following instruction:

Write "What if" at the top of your pads. Now list ten fantasy product–related ideas that complete the "What if" question.

In the session with the candy manufacturers, I offered these examples:

- What if all our competitors went out of business—what opportunities would that present?

- What if we could find out what the next big seller in the healthy snack category would be?

What-ifs yield some interesting ideas and serve as an effective stimulus for additional ideas. Here are some of the ideas that emerged from the candy manufacturing session:

- What if there was a pill that overweight people could take to lose their taste for sugar candies?

- What if there was a law requiring all candy makers to put warning labels on candy wrappers as on cigarette packages?

- What if we could produce transparent candies?

HOW TO KEEP THE IDEAS FLOWING

Groups don't run out of ideas—the window of opportunity through which to access the collective idea bank simply closes. As a facilitator, your job is to understand how to continually reopen that window with an inexhaustible supply of Ideation exercises. In Chapter 8, "Making It Happen," I'll show you how to create a wide variety of Ideation drills for stimulating the collective creative potential of a group.

Question Exercise

The Question Exercise is one of the most productive drills you can conduct during any workflow management session. I use this tool to enable session participants to expand their operating context or framing of an issue in order to transform their thinking and creative capabilities. In addition, it also provides a means for less outgoing individuals to be more courageous about expanding their intellectual and creative comfort zones.

During the Ideation phase, you'll normally conduct at least two rounds of Questions. After boarding each round, always ask the group for additional ideas. Two or three rounds of the Question Exercise usually generates dozens of fresh ideas.

With the candy manufacturer group, for example, I waited till participants returned from a break to launch the first Question Exercise of the day:

> Please take a clean sheet of paper and, without discussion, respond to the following: What question should we ask ourselves now? Please write down as many questions as you can think of. You have three minutes for this.

Occasionally someone asks, "What kind of question are you looking for?" My reply is standard: "Whatever question pops into your mind."

At the end of three minutes, I asked the group to stop and went around the room boarding just one question from each person. Some of the questions were quite thought-provoking; among them were:

- Are we looking for a snack that will appeal to kids only, to adults, or to both?

- Are we looking for a snack that will appeal to one sex more than the other?

- Are we looking for a snack that doesn't contain sugar?

- How are we defining *healthy*?

- What's the definition of *candy*?

- How about a new name for the product category?

- Why don't we create a new product category and own it?

Note that if participants think it's important to resolve a question in-session, I accommodate them. However, that doesn't mean I get involved in content. It's the group's responsibility to more clearly define the purpose of the session when necessary. At one point during the Question Exercise, the candy manufacturer group wanted to resolve some of the questions that had been raised, notably, "How are we defining *healthy*?" Not wanting to divert their creativity, I gave the group time to explore these questions in increments of five minutes. In that instance, my role was to be a scribe only.

In general, however, after you've displayed their first set of questions, and without any preamble, direct the group to ask a better question. Give them just one minute for this. If someone asks you to define what a "better" question would be, reply, "A *bigger* question." Discussing the exercise in further detail dilutes its effectiveness.

Here is a sample of the questions that emerged from the participants in the candy manufacturer Innovation Session:

- What are the ten top snack flavors for kids, teens, and adults?

- How do taste preferences differ by age group and sex?

- Will teens buy custom-wrapped snacks online?

- Would a public relations campaign about healthy snacks hurt current candy sales?

- Should our healthy snack line be positioned to have no tie-in with our current lines?

- Are we potentially shooting ourselves in the foot with an entry in the healthy snack category?

- What's the risk/reward reality if we launch a healthy line?

- Why not acquire a healthy snack line and apply our marketing expertise to grow the brand?

As before, collect and display the questions that result from this part of the exercise. Without pausing, again ask the participants to write three new ideas. For stimuli, suggest that they review the questions you've just boarded. Give them three minutes to do this.

The candy manufacturer participants responded with the following ideas:

- A package of cooked French fries with a hot sauce

- Candettes and Healthettes made from different veggies and fruits

- As a promotional tie-in with large health-oriented supermarket chains (such as Whole Foods), a snack product that we would manufacture and they would market under their house brand

- Girl Scout healthy snacks as a companion product to Girl Scout cookies

---

UNANSWERED QUESTIONS ARE VALUABLE

You will undoubtedly end up with more questions than answers from the Innovation Session. Remember that all unanswered questions become Information Gaps to be recorded and displayed for postsession resolution. This becomes fodder for additional formal and informal Innovation work sessions.

By the time I had run through more than ten cycles of Ideation with the candy manufacturer group, including a variety of creativity exercises as well as a series of Question Exercises, the group had produced between 400 and 500 new product ideas. (Often, the yield can exceed 600.) Understandably, many of those ideas were absolutely ridiculous, and a lot of them were incomplete. That was fine, because I knew they would serve to jump-start a productive Building phase—and we needed only one great idea to create a multi-billion-dollar brand.

Here are some of the ideas that the candy manufacturer Innovation Session yielded at the end of the Ideation phase:

- Designer snacks
- Snacks endorsed by fashion models

- Snacks wrapped in bumper stickers that you can put on your car

- A liquid candy

- A candy that's also good for pets

- A surprise snack that tastes different to each person who eats it

- A mystery snack—you don't know which of five different snacks you'll get

- Solid espresso snacks in three variations: black, with cream, and with toffee

- A tongue-in-cheek "prescription" snack line called "Just What the Doctor Ordered"

- Local school logo–wrapped snacks

- A special promotional giveaway snack line for kid's lemonade stands, culminating in the "youth entrepreneur of the summer"

- A scholarship-inside-the-wrapper promotion

- A new delivery system for healthy snacks that we create— such as a countertop health snack machine

You won't always have the need (or time) to conduct all of the exercises discussed in this step. However, you now have an idea of the many ways to leverage the creative potential of a group. After a couple of these sessions, you'll be able to switch fluidly from one Ideation exercise to another and create those magic moments when a group crackles with creativity and enthusiasm.

In the beginning, you may feel overwhelmed by the number

of new product ideas the group has generated. Don't be. Simply work the Building process and immerse yourself in the success of the group. If it's obvious you are enjoying yourself, the group will feed off your positive energy.

Phase Two: Building

You are now ready to bring the group into the second phase of the Innovation Session: the *Building* phase. The strategy of the Building phase is threefold:

1. Focus on ways to make ideas work.

2. Avoid any discussion about why the ideas might *not* work.

3. Convert raw ideas to concepts.

Ideas vs. Concepts

The difference between a new product idea and a new product concept is in the degree of completeness. A new product idea is often just a bare-bones hunch or an inkling of what might be possible; a new product concept, however, is an idea that has been fleshed out. Often, a new product concept reveals itself when several ideas are combined or when a value-added feature is integrated with an existing product or service.

A new product idea usually needs more attention (Building) before it is considered viable. Sometimes raw ideas are exposed in focus groups to find that missing piece of the puzzle that promotes a new idea to concept status. The spectrum of possibilities in new product development is limitless.

Allow the participants to take a break, and when they reconvene, explain to them this distinction between a new product idea and a concept. Point out that, for reference purposes, you've numbered all of the ideas they generated during the creativity exercises in the previous step. Although there will still be some overlap—people coming up with similar ideas—you'll see that you and the group have hundreds of new product ideas with which to work.

Stay Positive

For this step, again break the group into teams. Participants can take the initiative for who belongs to which team, but encourage them to try to form teams that are as different in their make-up as possible.

For this part of the session, tell the participants they are free to stand, sit, talk, and move about the room as freely as they wish. They may walk around the conference room and review all of the ideas on the walls. They may sit on the floor if they wish. Unlike the format of the previous team steps, in which the teams were strictly separated, in the Building phase there are no physical barriers between teams. Actually, the more they mingle, the more successful they'll be.

The assignment for each team is to use the ideas displayed on the walls to build discrete new product concepts—concepts that the teams believe their organization could market successfully. The teams get fifteen minutes to agree upon ten new product ideas. Some of the ideas they are starting with may already be complete new product concepts; some may just be partial ideas that, when combined with others, become concepts. Generally, there are many bits and scraps of ideas. Each team's task is to identify, develop, and build the ten best.

Encourage everyone to strive for creative collaboration by building upon each other's ideas, thoughts, questions, comments, and observations. Tell them to forget pride of authorship; this is not a competition. They are part of a creative team in this phase.

This creative collaboration includes continuing to consider the ridiculous and the absurd. Many great inventions and ideas were considered ridiculous or absurd at first—for example, the idea that the Earth was round. The goal in the Building phase is to flesh out all the ideas, including the ridiculous, and see if there is potential for a new product (or whatever the Innovation goal of a given session might be).

There is only one vital restriction: Everyone agrees that there will be *absolutely no negative evaluation during this step.* This phase of the session is just as creative as the Ideation phase that was just completed. The group has uncovered many new product possibilities that now need to be dealt with in a manner that ensures that (1) enough attention is given to each idea and (2) time is not wasted on ideas that don't have potential. Paradoxically, this can be accomplished by first focusing on opportunities for success as opposed to possibilities for failure. In other words, the group must now look at the "pros" of each idea, fleshing out the details, and not worry about the "cons."

If some participants forget and make comments about what's wrong with a particular idea or why it won't work, the other team members should politely remind them of the *no evaluation* agreement.

As in previous exercises, let the group know when they have five minutes left to go and again when they have thirty seconds left.

CIRCULATE

While the Building phase is in progress, it's important for the facilitator to circulate through the room. Visit each team several times and make sure there's no evaluation going on. Validate and encourage, but don't get in the way. Keep your comments to a minimum.

Team Display

When the time is up, instruct the teams to stop, and reassemble the participants as one group, seated or standing. Have someone from each team mount the new product concepts on the front wall. Request a volunteer from each team to read aloud that team's list. As the volunteers post their concepts, the other participants should be trying to write two new ideas based on the concepts being presented at the front of the room. Encourage the participants to ask for clarification from the scribes presenting each team's list of concepts.

To ensure the maximum interchange, instruct team scribes to articulate clearly and allow for input from their team members as well as questions from the floor. Don't let them rush through their lists; it's up to you to orchestrate the process so people have time to write new ideas.

When all of the teams have shared their output, ask them to expand or modify in any way their list of concepts. They can do this without returning to their team locations. Give them ten minutes for this, and then ask the entire group to share all new ideas. Board these ideas.

THE INNOVATION SESSION

You've probably noticed by now that I request that participants come up with new ideas at every opportunity. "Always be asking for new ideas" is the mantra of successful innovation.

The Innovation Session with the candy manufacturers group yielded the following output from the Building phase:

- New delivery systems such as online, custom-packaged (wrapped) health snacks

- Countertop custom wrapper machines

- Creation of a mini-dessert (dessertettes)

- Foreign dessert/snack/cereal combinations (à la Jamaican liquid porridge)

- Snacks reminiscent of types of Middle Eastern confections

- Dried seafood snacks

At this point, the group has completed the Building phase of the Innovation Session; the remainder of the time will be devoted to the Evaluation process and the Action Plan.

Speaking of time, it's going to be very much on your mind at this stage of any Innovation Session. However, both the Evaluation and the Action Plan can be completed in less than two hours—forty minutes for Evaluation and thirty minutes for the Action Plan. This is always a good time for a break.

While the group is on break, assign a number to each concept and idea that's been generated thus far. Use brightly colored markers for this, and eliminate blatant duplicates.

Phase Three: Evaluation

The Evaluation phase moves the participants from a focus on creativity to a focus on possibility and potential. Instead of coming up with as many ideas and concepts as possible, the goal of this phase is to evaluate each concept and identify those that are most likely to be successful.

At this point in the session, the terms *idea* and *concept* can be used interchangeably. The distinction between the two has served its purpose: In the first Ideation phase, we needed any ideas, even partial ones; then in the Building phase, we wanted the ideas to be fleshed out (or connected to other ideas) to create complete concepts. Invoking the differences between concept and idea during the Evaluation phase is more of a hindrance than a help, since the wall is now covered with ideas, concepts, and everything in between.

For the sake of simplicity, I'll use the term *concept* for the remainder of this chapter, with the understanding that ideas that might not technically qualify as concepts may still be considered.

JUDGE, BUT STAY POSITIVE

The Evaluation phase of the session is performed with an upbeat, innovative spirit. By that I mean don't let the atmosphere of innovation deteriorate and become driven by a mindset that says, "Let's see how many of these ideas we can eliminate." This is an opportunity to guide the group in a manner that utilizes a creative attitude to do a cognitive (rational and logical thinking)

> job—a critical workflow management skill in an organization committed to a culture of innovation.

Assessing the Concepts

To create a "short list" of concepts, first make sure that all of the proposed concepts are clear to all participants. Read aloud the first concept (on the list) and confirm that everyone understands it. Working quickly, do the same for every concept displayed on the wall. Allow dialogue for purposes of clarification only.

At this point, your goal is to assist the group to identify the most viable new product concepts. Pattern recognition is a useful tool to employ for this. Suggest to participants that they look at the big picture before getting into details. Ask them to review all of the ideas and identify patterns or interconnectivities that spark their interest. For example, does a particular concept build on previous new product successes?

Once everyone is clear about the proposed concepts, it's time to do a critical assessment of each one. Tell the group that you'll be pointing to one concept at a time, and you would like their input on the viability of each concept. Basically, the goal is to determine whether that particular concept is something that, in the opinion of the participants, has potential as a new product for the organization. For example, with regard to idea #1: Is it indeed a new product concept or just an idea that needs more work? Can it be developed into a viable new product concept? Can it be combined with any other concepts? Do we want to spend any more time on this?

Maintain a brisk pace for this step, since there is a multitude of new product concepts and ideas to assess. You can't spend more time than is absolutely necessary on each concept or idea. If you spend too much time on any one concept, the group loses momentum and energy. On the other hand, make sure you don't throw out the baby with the bathwater by not spending enough time to recognize a great idea.

If necessary, make notations in color next to concepts for later reference. Allow the group to help you capture the essence of all new product concepts. Remind participants that this is the payoff step of the Innovation Session; by the time they finish this phase, they'll have many new product concepts ranging in viability from "interesting" to "exciting."

When a large number of new product ideas have been generated, some participants may express concern about "losing" some good ideas during the Evaluation phase. Assure them that a list of all the partial ideas, complete ideas, and concepts will be written up and distributed to participants within twenty-four hours after the conclusion of the session.

TOO MANY CONCEPTS?

When you're running a session and get to this step, don't become discouraged or nervous if you run out of time; you can always reconvene to finish the job of concept assessment. What a nice problem to create: too many new product ideas to evaluate in one session!

Top Ten

Once participants have identified concepts that appear to have strong appeal, guide them in ranking these concepts in terms of their viability. Specifically, ask them to take a sheet of paper and, without discussion, list their top ten new product concept choices. Give them ten minutes to do this.

When the time is up, solicit each person's top ten list of concepts. Each time a concept appears on someone's individual top ten list, place a check mark next to that concept on the master list displayed at the front of the room. When you've accounted for everyone's selections, count the check marks and give each concept a total score.

Record the top twenty concepts on a separate sheet. In the opinion of the group, these product concepts are worthy of consideration by the decision makers in the organization. Typically, most of them will undergo some type of qualitative concept testing, for example, with focus groups. Concepts with the strongest viability feedback would subsequently be scheduled for quantitative testing.

Phase Four: The Action Plan

The final step in the process is to develop an Action Plan to document the Innovation Session output in an actionable format with Tasks, Responsibilities, and Due Dates. In the session with the candy manufacturer group, the top twenty concepts were promoted to Action Plan status.

These are some of the concepts that drew attention in our case study session:

- A liquid oatmeal drink
- Middle Eastern confections (variations on dates, figs, and Turkish delight)
- Customized snack wrappers
- A countertop dispenser for warm snacks, to be placed in stores
- A line of ethnic snacks with a "healthy" spin for distribution by grocery stores in ethnic neighborhoods
- Vitamin-infused snacks that taste good to kids

In addition to the Next Steps already mentioned (qualitative and quantitative concept testing), some product concepts were assigned to specific individuals for follow-up. The research and development manager, for example, wanted input from other members of that department. Often, if a food product prototype can be inexpensively produced, concept testing includes a taste test.

An Action Plan is also important for key decision makers who were not present at the Innovation Session and, therefore, require detailed session feedback to enable them to make informed decisions. Likewise, outside suppliers such as an advertising agency may be brought into the loop and assigned specific tasks based on the Innovation Session—more specifically, on the Action Plan resulting from the Innovation Session.

New product ideas that didn't make the cut are written up, edited for clarity, and distributed to all participants for further review.

Once the top new product concepts and Information Gaps have been accounted for in the Action Plan, you have completed the Innovation Session.

FINAL THOUGHTS ON THE INNOVATION SESSION

Every Innovation Session you conduct is unique, even if you work with the same group of individuals each time. This is because of the structural flexibility and the spectrum of options available to you within each of the collaborative sessions. The session with the candy manufacturers group included a number of exercises designed to access and leverage the creative capabilities of a roomful of mostly cognitive-mind types. Once you and others on your team become familiar with the collaborative sessions, you can use the processes in an à la carte fashion. That level of workflow management capability enables you to create more value for the organization.

While the strategy underlying all the Ideation exercises is the same—to enable session participants to stop thinking and start imagining—the means to accomplish this skill are unlimited. The best way to understand this is to frame the procedure as a two-step process: distraction of rational thought and accessing of creative capabilities. This can be achieved simply by adhering to the workflow session structure.

As mentioned earlier, there is a paradoxical element to all of this in that we're using structure to access creativity; the Innovation Session structure is primarily the act of separating two collaboration dynamics: freewheeling creative Ideation and thoughtful Evaluation.

Chapter 4

THE PROBLEM-SOLVING SESSION

*The significant problems we face cannot be
solved at the same level of thinking we were
at when we created them.*
—ALBERT EINSTEIN

Most of the problems we encounter in the conduct of
organizational management are solvable. The reason
we find many of them a challenge is that we try to solve
them in conventional meetings, using conventional thinking processes. The Problem-Solving Session produces
transformative outcomes because it's an innovation-driven
process; we don't try to cognitively hammer out solutions.
Instead, we create an environment that entices the solution
to reveal itself. This process upgrades the ability of a group
to solve problems utilizing a unique blend of cognitive and
creative skills.

WHEN TO USE THE PROBLEM-SOLVING SESSION

The following is a partial list of specific needs that would benefit from the use of a Problem-Solving Session:

- Facilitating intradepartmental involvement in the resolution of a problem

- Obtaining input from key individuals with regard to a specific problem, such as a systems and procedures upgrade

- Enabling managers and supervisors to operate from a unified strategic perspective

- Delegating Problem-Solving downward and horizontally

- Fostering earlier ownership for issues across departments and disciplines

- Encouraging early (proactive) Problem-Solving activities as a strategy to curtail the development of critical issues

- Upgrading the Problem-Solving capabilities of managers, supervisors, and their staffs

- Resolving issues related to exponential change and economic uncertainty (such as online alternatives to traditional industry delivery vehicles, target audience segmentation, brand erosion, constricting budgets, global competition, capital goods and equipment upgrades, and cultural adjustments as a consequence of mergers and acquisitions)

While Problem-Solving has much in common with Innovation, as you'll see, it's a more inclusive process to the extent that significant emphasis is placed on leveraging the rational or cognitive capabilities of a group in addition to harnessing the group's creative potential.

SESSION LOGISTICS

You can conduct a Problem-Solving Session with as many as twenty people, although I recommend a smaller group for your first session. Six to ten people would be ideal. After that, size won't matter to you.

There's really no definitive way to estimate how long it will take a group to solve a problem, or several problems. Sometimes the most complex problems get resolved in a matter of minutes; other times it takes longer. So, in the beginning, decide how much time you're going to allocate—for example, one hour—and request that your participants keep an additional hour in reserve. After the first session, you'll be much more confident about estimating the time allotment.

The best time of day to run a Problem-Solving Session is first thing in the morning. I don't schedule Problem-Solving Sessions for the late afternoon if I can possibly avoid it. (Fatigue impairs the ability to make sound decisions and wise choices.) When possible, I'll opt to reconvene a late-running Problem-Solving Session the following morning.

THE CASE STUDY

The CEO of a leading high-end cosmetics organization was concerned about the growing number of problems that had the organization in a permanent state of emergency. Minor issues that needed timely handling were routinely left unaddressed until they became serious problems; everyone could demonstrate they had a challenging workload and were not part of the problem; turnover of middle managers and supervisors was at its highest in the company's history.

In an effort to cope, managers had adopted crisis management work habits and were spending their time putting out fires. They no longer addressed core workflow responsibilities such as upgrading systems and procedures, training, proactive customer service, and new product development. The situation was time sensitive and required resolution to avoid domino-like consequences. My assignment was to identify the cause of the problem and fix it.

I met with a twelve-person group that included the CEO and her senior executives. We had allocated a one-day work session with the usual caveat: Keep calendars clear in case we needed more time.

The Problem-Solving Session

Step One: Laying the Groundwork

As in all work sessions, the first step is to establish an agreement with the group regarding your role and theirs. Emphasize that you are responsible for the process—structuring and guiding them through the session—but they are responsible for content.

As part of laying the groundwork for the meeting, also explain to the group the importance of capturing Information Gaps that arise during the session. Write the heading "Information Gaps" at the top of one of the easels to emphasize your intention to record any unanswered questions that arise during the session.

Step Two: Identify the Problem

Once the rules and parameters of the sessions have been explained and all the logistics are in place, the next step is to identify the core problem that will be at the center of the session.

Begin by writing your understanding of the problem on an easel. Then, guided by the group, edit your description of the problem to the satisfaction of the group. Don't strive for perfection—it isn't necessary at this point. Your goal is to get general agreement that the problem statement is in the ballpark of reality. When you think you've achieved this, mount the page that documents the problem on the wall. In a normal situation, try not to spend more than five minutes on this step.

Sometimes it helps if the group attempts to simplify what appears to be a complex problem by breaking it down into a set of smaller problems that might be easier to solve. One clue that this is necessary is when you notice that the group is having difficulty agreeing on the definition of a problem. If you suspect this is the case, address the group as follows:

> Please review the original problem, and let's see if it can be understood better as a group of smaller problems. To save time, I'm going to function as the scribe for the group and write up your ideas. Let's see how many sub-problems we can identify. Take five minutes for this.

Display all of the subproblems on the board and then ask the group to reframe the original problem as two or three discrete, smaller problems. Give the group approximately three minutes to do this, and add the new problem statements to the board.

When you're working with several seemingly unrelated problems, mount all of them on separate sheets and ask the group to look for patterns and interconnectivities. That way, you'll be able to reduce the number of original problems by combining, editing, clarifying, restating, and so forth, which in some cases actually triggers the appearance of solutions very early in the process.

To jump-start things with the cosmetic company participants, I ran a brief Issues Management Session to get the maximum amount of information in the shortest period of time (see Chapter 2, "The Issues Management Session"). I then switched gears, shifted to a Problem-Solving Session, and guided the group to a consensus about the fundamental problem. In this instance, we got agreement on the following problem statement:

> How do we reduce the number of emergency issues in all departments and across all disciplines within the organization?

BREAKING A RULE

The only time I deal with content during any workflow management session is when I'm helping a group come to an agreement about the definition of the problem at the start of a Problem-Solving Session. My role in such instances is that of

---

scribe for the group. Specifically, I write what they tell me to write. However, while in that role I'm mentally composing what I think they mean as an appropriate problem statement. This is dangerous territory for any facilitator.

I give myself only five minutes to accomplish this step. And while I'm merely acting as their scribe, I stay in firm control of the group because some people may be attempting to influence the wording of the problem to satisfy their personal agenda.

Once I have general agreement on a statement of the problem, I rewrite it for legibility, mount it at the front of the conference room, and allow the group to direct me to edit it to their satisfaction. I'm striving only for general agreement during this step.

Step Three: Reframe the Problem

As mentioned previously, the Problem-Solving Session depends as much on creative thinking as on cognitive skills, such as the ability to analyze data and form rational and logical conclusions from that data. The process for resolving problems, therefore, includes a number of creativity exercises, such as the ones introduced in the Innovation Session.

The first exercise you will use is the What-If Exercise. This exercise allows the group to uncover different facets of the problem and, in the process, some possible solutions, by turning the core problem into a "What if . . .?" statement.

Once the group has agreed on the core problem, ask the participants to take five minutes to write as many interpretations of this problem (or its solution) as possible, without any discussion among themselves. They can take poetic license to be as expansive or specific as they wish, but they must preface their restatements of the problem with "What if."

They have only five minutes for the exercise. At the conclusion, ask each participant to share his or her list.

For the Problem-Solving Session with the cosmetics company group, I gave the participants some examples of what I was looking for:

- *What if* we were more proactive in our overall workflow management skills?
- *What if* we motivated managers and supervisors to adopt a team mentality?
- *What if* we identified the root cause of our mounting number of Critical Issues?
- *What if* we determined where there's a concentration of Critical Issues and why this is so?

At the end of the five minutes, participants had produced a number of perspectives on the fundamental problem for the cosmetics company, using this format:

- What if we had better lines of communication?
- What if we had enough people to keep up with our expanding workload?
- What if we had a positive corporate culture?
- What if we handled problems by fixing instead of blaming?
- What if we spent less time in unproductive meetings?

- What if we had more personnel stability? As soon as people are trained for one job they are moved to another spot needing a quick fix.

DIG BELOW THE SURFACE

Not settling for the initial problem (the surface problem) is an effective way to identify more deeply rooted systemic problems and issues. Once you have boarded the problem, ask the group to take five minutes to write down different root causes and issues that they believe might contribute to the problem. After five minutes, collect one root cause or issue from each participant and display it on the easel.

Here's a sampling of the outcome of this step from the cosmetic company's session:

- There's a big disconnect between the frontline managers and the executives to whom they report.
- There are murmurs of a "lack of respect of upper management."
- We have poor interdepartmental communications ("It's easier to do it myself than to delegate and have to explain things").
- We have poor intradepartmental collaboration ("I never know what they're doing until I get a complaint from a retailer").
- Phantom protocols abound (there's no time to do things properly").

> - There are lots of complaints from major department stores regarding promotions, displays, out-of-stocks, and co-op advertising allocation.

Step Four: Ask for Solutions

Once you've conducted several rounds of the What-If Exercise and have identified some of the roots of the problem you are addressing, you can make your first request for solutions. Instruct the group to write three possible solutions to the problem, without discussion. Give them five minutes for this exercise.

When their time is up, go around the room and display one solution from each person. When all of the solutions have been displayed, ask the group, "Do we have a solution to the problem?"

If any group indicates that they've found a solution, display it, with the group's editorial input, and determine whether there is consensus. If there is agreement that a solution has been found, you can proceed directly to Step Seven: the Action Plan.

REMEMBER TO CLARIFY

As in all the sessions, your job as a facilitator is to make sure the thinking of the participants is completely and accurately reflected in what is written on the boards. Never hesitate to clarify where appropriate, and always confirm that the author of any new offering agrees that his or her submission has been boarded correctly.

Step Five: Expand the Search

A solution rarely presents itself from the first request. More likely, a series of creativity exercises—including the vitally important Question Exercise—will be necessary before the group can identify a solution or solutions.

Exactly which exercises you use and how many you need will be different for each group and each session. The cosmetic company required a lengthy Problem-Solving Session to arrive at viable solutions. Next, we explore some of the creativity exercises that you may want to use in your own sessions, employing examples from the cosmetic company.

Question Exercise

As you can imagine, the Question Exercise plays a starring role in Problem-Solving Sessions, since the process enables participants to both expand and focus their perspectives—in other words, to see the bigger picture in some cases and to take notice of overlooked details in others. As a consequence, their problem-solving capability improves because they learn how to reframe issues, conditions, and trends. (It also makes it easier for more reticent participants to go beyond their intellectual courage zones.)

Ask each participant to write the word "Questions" at the top of a fresh sheet of paper and respond to the following:

What question do we need to ask ourselves at this time?

Give the group three minutes to finish the assignment. Then go around the room and take one question from each person. Write these questions on an easel and, *without* addressing the questions, instruct the group as follows:

Write a better question. You have one minute. Please start.

Repeat the process of taking just one question per person and displaying each question on the board. Naturally, there will be some overlap and duplication of questions. You can handle such duplication by placing check marks next to questions that have already been submitted. You now have a list of many questions that are related, in varying degrees, to the problem displayed on the easel at the front of the room.

Asking for a better question is a key element of this exercise. For example, with the cosmetic company group, I began to suspect that the issue that people were not taking early responsibility wasn't because of the workload but was a consequence of a more fundamental cause: *dysfunctional workflow management habits spawned in the very meetings used for collaboration.*

It became obvious to me that little collaboration was achieved in these meetings for all the obvious reasons: Bosses ran the meetings, content and process were not kept separate, there was lots of unproductive brainstorming but no Action Plans and no attention to Information Gaps, and there was a general resentment about the time wasted in these meetings. I also inferred that senior executives avoided culpability for any of this and that they had isolated the CEO from knowledge of what was happening in the trenches.

To get confirmation of what I suspected to be the underlying cause of the problem, I conducted a series of Question Exercises to force the group to dig deeper. Here are some of the questions they came up with:

- Is this problem occurring in our second-tier retail outlets?
- Are we having these problems in other countries?
- Are we getting any consumer feedback?
- How soon before we'll see erosion in our share of market?

I boarded the first round of questions; then, instead of addressing any of them, I challenged the group to ask a better question. After some grumbling (which I completely ignored), they went back to the drawing board. I gave them an additional three minutes for this round, and here are some of the questions that resulted:

- Is our competition having the same problems we're having?
- Did we do exit interviews with the key people we lost?
- Do we know the real reason they left?
- Have we identified all of the problems?
- Are we in for some more surprises?
- Should we meet with some of our top department store personnel and ask them how we can do a better job?

You'll notice that the questions were becoming more solution-oriented and that Information Gaps were beginning to sprout.

I boarded these questions, again resisting the urge to address any of them, and pushed the group into a third round. Here's a sample of what that round produced:

- Are our problems solvable?

- Are we avoiding some core issues here?

- Do we have a communication breakdown within departments, between departments, and across all disciplines?

- Are our problems a consequence of attitudes or lack of skills, or both?

- Are we, as a group, committed to changing these problems?

With each series of questions, the group moves closer to the solution. Highly leveraged questions, such as "Are our problems a consequence of attitudes or lack of skills or both?," usually lead to the root causes of the problems.

It's possible that the solution to the problem has manifested itself. This is why it is important throughout the session to continually ask the participants whether they see a solution to the problem—or whether they think they can now build a solution. There are several exercises you can use to maximize the participants' solution-building efforts.

Solution Exercise

After a series of What-If and Question exercises, it's possible that someone in the room already has what they consider to be the solution or part of the solution to the problem, or that each of several people has a different piece of a solution, or that the solution is already mounted on the wall in the form of a question. Give participants five minutes to check out this possibility, instructing them as follows:

Without discussion, please scan all the questions mounted on the walls to determine if we have a solution, or part of a solution, or a pattern that implies a solution.

At the end of the five-minute period, instruct the group to stop writing and ask them, "How many people believe we have a solution to the problem?" (This is similar to an Innovation Session, where you're always asking for additional ideas.)

Board all possible solutions and parts of solutions, and number them. Then point to each solution and ask for a show of hands in response to this question "How many people think this is a solution or a partial solution?" Record all votes for solutions and partial solutions. If the group thinks a solution has been found, write that solution on your easel in as much detail as possible. Do the same for any other potential solutions.

Team Solution Exercise

In many situations, it's better to break the groups into teams that can collaborate on possible solutions. These teams shouldn't be too large—maybe a maximum of five people. Make sure the teams are isolated from each other as much as possible. Instruct each team to elect someone to function as scribe to record the team's solutions and partial solutions on the easel.

Once the teams have been formed, instruct them as follows:

Using all of the questions, partial solutions, and discussion with your team members as stimuli, build a solution to the problem. First develop your own solution or partial solution and then collaborate with your team members to build on each other's ideas, suggestions, and solutions.

As with the individual-based solution-building, give the teams fifteen minutes to identify any solutions that may have emerged. Then bring the teams back together for a full group discussion. As before, request one representative from each team to display the team's solutions, and assign a number to each solution. Ask the representatives to explain the team's rationale for the solution produced.

When all of the team representatives are finished, ask participants to review the proposed solutions and decide whether they have a solution to their problem. Allow this open discussion to continue for approximately ten minutes. This time you will be the scribe for the group, so request of them: "Please tell me what to write."

Note that when you give participants the freedom to communicate with one another, you must ensure that the process is productive. Never hesitate to call it to their attention when they are not being productive. The most typical problem is everyone talking at the same time, and, ironically, this happens most often with high-energy, productive groups. Your challenge is to orchestrate a balance between chaos and productivity.

KNOW WHEN TO STOP

At the end of each cycle, take a reading of the energy level of the group and how much time is available. Sometimes, a single,

---

complex problem can take more time to resolve than anticipated. This can happen for a variety of reasons; two of the most common are group fatigue and time constraints. Always be tuned in to the physical and emotional dynamics of your group; let them know that their comfort level is a priority to you, and allow yourself to be guided by them for frequency of breaks and session duration.

If a group is having trouble identifying the solution to a particular problem and they've been at it for some time, a creativity exercise (see the next text section) will stir up the creative juices. However, don't try to run a group on "empty."

Creative Solution-Building

As a means to invigorate a stalled Problem-Solving Session, an Ideation exercise recharges the dynamics in the conference room and status quo thinking is replaced by creative speculation unrelated to the task of solving the problem. The following is an example of one of these creativity exercises. (Others can be found in Chapter 3, "The Innovation Session," as well as in Chapter 8, "Making It Happen.")

Ask the group to use a clean sheet of paper to respond to the following, without discussion:

Imagine how your life would change if you—and only you—could fly. You would have no wings or any other apparatus; you would simply have the ability to levitate at will and travel thousands of miles in any direction you choose at the altitude you prefer. You've just discovered this ability, and no one else knows about it. You have no idea why you have this ability or what it means. Please take ten minutes to write down what you would do with this capability.

Although such flights of fancy may seem ridiculous, the goal is to help groups get outside their everyday problem-solving zones and address problems from an unrelated and more flexible perspective.

After ten minutes, go around the room and ask each person for a thirty-second summation of their response to the exercise. Don't board any of this information, however. Instead, while the creative group window is open and the mood is light, give participants three minutes to write down—without discussion—two solutions to the problem that the group is working on.

When the time is up, ask them to stop writing and board their proposed solutions. When all these solutions are boarded, ask the group to review them and determine whether there is a solution to the problem. If the participants think a solution has manifested itself, assist them to write it up and board it. Once there's agreement from the group that a solution has been uncovered, you can proceed to the Action Plan step.

One of your primary responsibilities as a facilitator is to create an environment that makes it easy for people to break out of their habitual thinking patterns. Once they do this, they will become effective problem solvers.

STRIKE WHILE THE IRON IS HOT

When you decide to utilize an Ideation exercise option, remember to minimize the time gap between the Ideation process and the request-for-solution step that follows. More specifically, when you complete an Ideation exercise, immediately ask the group to write two or three additional solutions to the problem.

The reason for this is to capitalize on the cognitive "interruption" that's just been created by the Ideation exercise. Be assured, the window of innovative opportunity is normally quite short before the relapse to habitual thinking occurs.

Cosmetic Company: The Path to a Solution

During the Problem-Solving Session with the cosmetics company, I used several solution-building exercises in an effort to guide the group toward a solution to the core problem of ownership and collaboration. The breakthrough occurred after a second series of questions had covered the walls of the conference room with a wide range of questions related to the problem.

I sensed then that the time was ripe for a change of pace. I boarded all questions and asked the group to break into three teams of four persons each. I gave participants only three minutes for this transition into teams, then I instructed them to come to an agreement, as a team, on the core problem that was suggested by all of the questions that had been asked.

I urged them to forget about trying to identify a solution and simply focus on identifying a single underlying problem or a group of related problems. They were free to talk to each other and walk around the room to review all the information mounted on the walls. I suggested that they elect a group scribe, and reminded them to look for patterns and interconnectivities. Each scribe would record the results from that team. I gave them fifteen minutes for this task.

While the teams worked, I circulated, making myself available for any process-related questions. (There weren't any—people were totally involved in the task at hand.) At the end of the fifteen minutes, I asked the group to reassemble, standing or seated, but to stay in their team clusters.

Each team representative mounted the respective team's results sheet and explained their conclusions about the underlying problem or group of problems. The following is a sampling of what each team presented.

Team A: Everything we're discussing is related to our management skills. The workloads are unevenly dispersed, and those of us with the most experience carry the heaviest loads. We're the ones who have to solve the problems because others didn't take ownership when it was a run-of-the-mill issue.

Team B: We're under the effect of an overwhelming number of critical issues and need to work every Saturday until we get them resolved. We need fewer meetings, less complaining, and more "doing."

The people we've hired to replace those who quit are still learning our systems and procedures, which need to be upgraded anyway. They're learning how to do things the way we do them, so nothing will change. It's absurd. We're caught in a vicious cycle.

Team C: We're operating in a culture of fear. As individuals, each of us is determined not to be the one left without a chair when the music stops. That attitude is keeping us from being proactive.

We're afraid to take ownership of issues, because it's too risky and we're already over our heads with the workloads we have. Our culture is the problem.

People don't do what they agree to do on time. And it's always someone else's fault. Communication has broken down and ownership is avoided at all costs.

What-If Exercise

Instead of spending time on further discussion about how bad things were, I changed gears again. I asked the group to complete the next step without discussion:

Please write "What if" at the top of a clean page and below that write down as many fantasy solutions to the problems we've just been discussing as you possibly can. For example, "What if all of our problems were wiped out, and tomorrow we got to start the day with none of the problems we now have?"

Here's another example: "What if, starting tomorrow, everybody took the time to be interested in how they could help make work easier for at least one other person in that department or any other department?"

I gave them ten minutes for this exercise. When the time was up, I took one "What if" at a time from each person and boarded all of them. Here's a sampling:

- What if everyone was willing to take early responsibility for issues related in any way to their area of responsibility?

- What if communication within and between departments was streamlined?

- What if everybody had the information they needed, on time, to do their jobs properly?

- What if people were no longer afraid of taking reasonable risks in an effort to create more value for the company?

- What if everyone's management skills improved significantly?

- What if people managed from a proactive perspective?

- What if the working atmosphere was positive and enjoyable?

- What if managers and executives validated and empowered others?

- What if there was no longer that vague disconnect in communication between upper and middle management?

- What if people were smiling instead of frowning?

- What if meetings were productive and enjoyable like what we're doing today?

- What if people enjoyed working for the company?

- What if our reputation with department stores was that we were the most professional and dependable cosmetics brand in the industry?

The change in attitude and energy in the conference room was palpable. To capitalize on it, I gave the participants the following instruction:

THE PROBLEM-SOLVING SESSION

Please go back to your team locations and come to an agreement on three possible solutions to transform the quality of workflow management in your organization. You have ten minutes. Please start.

When they reassembled, I asked the team scribes to present their solution lists and mount them on the board. Here's what they recommended:

Team A:

- Provide management skills training to all managers and supervisors.
- Empower managers to be proactive.
- Take the time to properly train new hires.

Team B:

- Streamline communications within and between departments.
- Upgrade workflow management systems and procedures at headquarters.
- Launch an initiative, led by senior management, to repair department store relations at every level (including CEO involvement).

Team C:

- Have senior executives become more involved in workflow management issues (i.e., validating and empowering all managers and supervisors).

- Repair the disconnect in communication between upper and middle management.

- Teach all managers and supervisors how to run Issues Management and Problem-Solving sessions.

Step Six: The Action Plan

As with the Issues Management and Innovation sessions, it is vital to capture all of the Information Gaps, Conclusions, and Next Steps from the session into an Action Plan. In the case of the cosmetics company, it was agreed that all of the suggested team solutions would be implemented, and an Action Plan was created specifying Next Steps, Responsibilities, and Due Dates. This provided transparency and responsibility and ensured ownership of issues.

To seed the conversion from meetings to workflow sessions, a group of key managers and supervisors volunteered to learn how to run Issues Management Sessions to replace meetings. That was accomplished in one day.

The results were transformative, and the Issues Management training was adopted by personnel across all departments and disciplines. This enabled systems and procedures to be streamlined, and crisis management work habits were dropped. The culture was rejuvenated, and the organization maintained its sterling reputation within the industry.

DON'T OVERDO IT

All of the workflow management sessions we've discussed are designed for the fast pace and interconnectivities of twenty-first-century organizational management. However, there's a line beyond which you should not go in your efforts to encourage someone to "let it all hang out."

You're in the process of learning transformative collaborative processes that involve participants learning to expand both their cognitive and their creative capabilities as a means to solve problems in an innovative manner. Some people's comfort zones will be challenged by this.

So be empathetic: Even one person with a negative or fearful attitude can compromise a workflow session. You have the knowledge and skills at your disposal to prevent this from happening; when combined with wisdom and sensitivity, you're well equipped to motivate, validate, and handle any situation you'll encounter in a manner that satisfies everyone's best interests.

Chapter 5

THE ONGOING PLANNING PROCESS

Historically, strategy planning was a scheduled affair, conducted yearly, semiannually, or quarterly by a handful of senior executives. It was usually held off-premises, and most managers didn't participate. In the digital age, this approach to strategic planning is obsolete. Economic and societal dynamics are changing too quickly for planning sessions based on a snapshot of the way things are.

Conventional strategy planning lost relevance for a lot of reasons: In addition to the fact that strategic intentions were routinely outdated by the time implementation was addressed, most organizations didn't have the wherewithal to deploy their intellectual and creative talent to reframe planning to counter exponential change. As a consequence, while preemptive opportunities abound in the digital economy, there's less time to score a preemptive strike.

Since all players now have access to the same information, the speed with which a management team identifies opportunities and converts them to value defines effective strategy.

To stay current, innovation and speed-to-market capabilities must be valued as core competencies, and the ability to leverage human capital more effectively must be a strategic imperative.

Bottom line, to be effective in the digital age, the time span between planning and implementation must be minimized. Accomplishing this has to be an ongoing process that (1) capitalizes on the interconnectivities created by technologies and (2) maximizes speed-to-market capabilities.

This has created the need to reframe the planning function from a scheduled event executed by a few to an ongoing process that involves many in order to leverage the cognitive and creative capabilities of in-house talent, to stay current in the face of exponential change, and to shorten the timeline between intentions, strategies, and implementation.

This chapter explains how planning can be developed and implemented by managers from all levels and disciplines within the organization. Core strategies are stripped-down, built-for-speed processes that can quickly adapt to change. The facilitating process for all of this is workflow sessions that unshackle collaboration from the limitations of outdated meeting practices and do a better job of leveraging human capital. The outcome is a real-time alternative to conventional planning that ensures the following:

- Planning input is ongoing, fluid, and multidirectional.
- All managers operate from a unified strategic perspective.
- Implementation times are minimized.
- Speed to market is maximized.

- Intellectual and creative capital is effectively leveraged.

- Organizational culture is defined by a mindset that values innovation and speed to market as means to manage change and create sustainable value.

THE THREE DRIVERS OF ONGOING PLANNING

Effective Ongoing Planning is driven by three interrelated dynamics:

1. Innovative collaboration practices
2. A robust Planning Database
3. Personal Workflow Planners

Innovative Collaboration Practices

As seen in Figure 5.1, outcomes from the three collaboration sessions (Issues Management, Innovation, and Problem-Solving) in the form of Action Plans are fed to a Planning Database at the conclusion of every workflow management session. This process creates critical-path transitioning from collaboration to Ongoing Planning.

A Robust Planning Database

The Planning Database is fed, primarily, by Action Plans and functions as the intelligence nerve center of the organi-

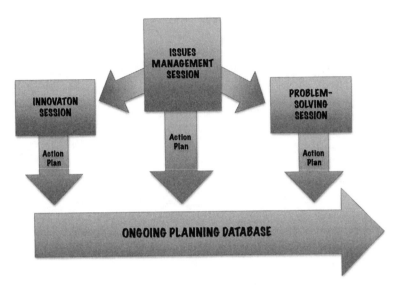

Figure 5.1   Workflow management system.

zation. Action Plans, in turn, function as the cohesive factor for Ongoing Planning, since they reflect and document outcomes from all workflow management sessions that occur within the organization. Thus, the Planning Database provides senior management the means to evaluate the integrity of workflow management practices and priorities in relation to marketplace realities.

The architecture of the Planning Database is customized to enable senior management to identify and assess interconnectivities, patterns, and trends in a variety of contexts and to monitor both the workflow of the organization and the heartbeat of the marketplace in real time. The Planning Database also functions as sonar for preemptive opportunities.

A planning coordinator monitors the database. This individual's job is to extrapolate strategically pertinent information from the Action Plans and other sources of competitive and market data. All managers utilize the database to identify collaborative opportunities and interconnectivities that create value and to ensure they're operating from a unified strategic perspective. Input by individual managers is encouraged in the form of Information Gap queries, initiative updates, intradepartmental task and project coordination, and so forth.

One of the advantages of this process is the availability of outcomes from all workflow management sessions conducted in the organization. Action Plans from past Innovation Sessions are used to jump-start scheduled sessions. A review of related Problem-Solving Sessions minimizes "reinventing-the-wheel" occurrences and maximizes outcomes from ongoing sessions. As a learning and training resource, the database is invaluable.

The Ongoing Planning Database is a vital component of best workflow management practices for two reasons:

1. **It is comprehensive:** All of the outcomes, from unanswered questions and unresolved issues to solutions, new concepts, and innovations, are captured and carefully organized to allow immediate access to everyone in the organization.

2. **It is ongoing:** Since data and information are updated in real time, a manager can, for example, track the progress of a new product introduction from an unlimited range of perspectives or get an up-to-date reading on target audience segmentation trends.

The database is the intelligence resource for detail on issues such as unresolved problems, possible solutions, Information Gaps, innovation initiatives, new product pipeline inventory, new product introduction tracking, and systems and procedures upgrades. For example, an executive responsible for coordinating intradepartmental workflow management activities would use the database as a starting point to avoid unnecessary duplication of effort; a brand manager in need of up-to-date competitive and marketplace activities would do likewise. In effect, the database serves as the key knowledge resource for all managers to access information on all facets of the organization, marketplace, and competition.

Personal Workflow Planners

Digital Workflow Planners are used by managers to handle expanding personal workloads and to streamline workflow management practices. The planners enable managers to maintain a strategic perspective as they manage issues, innovate, and solve problems.

Workflow Planners are not submitted to the Planning Database. They are a personal workflow tool that managers may customize to fit their individual leadership styles. Used in combination with the collaborative protocols, the Workflow Planners sharpen strategic awareness and ensure a manager's ability to leverage the intellectual and creative capabilities of others.

One tendency of good managers is to be first in line to volunteer for additional responsibilities. While the positives of this far outnumber the negatives, we need to remember that busy managers adopt crisis management work habits in an effort to stay current with expanding workloads. Crisis management work habits are in place when managers are spending a significant amount of their time "putting out fires" and neglecting core workflow tasks such as upgrading systems and procedures, business development, training, and ensuring impeccable customer service. Workflow Planners prevent this from happening by enabling managers to upgrade from the conventional to-do list mentality to a strategic and more proactive mindset.

For instance, one of the easiest issues for busy managers to overlook is the resolution of an Information Gap. Often, the timely resolution of a particular Information Gap has organization-wide pertinence. For example, a personnel department supervisor (in a Problem-Solving Session) wondered how other companies in the same industry handled the problem of sick-day peaks and valleys, which was an issue in certain departments within the organization since productivity was often impaired and stress escalated when key employees missed work.

In the course of resolving the Information Gap, it was discovered that their biggest competitor had solved the problem with a vigorous commitment to cross-training. The competitor had achieved this by means of a simple two-step process:

1. All job categories underwent critical-path scrutiny to identify which employee absences created the most negative consequences.

2. These employees then trained two others to do their jobs.

The company emulated the competitor's process, and the result was so successful that it gradually expanded the program to include all of its key positions. Today, every person in the company is capable of wearing two hats. And because this program was introduced properly, as an empowerment of each individual, morale skyrocketed and a systemic problem was resolved.

AN OPERATIONAL TOOL

The database is more than an information source, however. It is an organic resource that is used by managers and executives from all levels and disciplines to develop and implement strategic initiatives.

At the operational level, for example, the database helps human resource managers to monitor the human capital needs of the company. Managers can use the information to monitor and assess workflow management performance and take preemptive action to improve productivity on the individual and business unit levels.

Historically, one of the key functions of top management was to ensure a unified strategic perspective at every level of the organization and across all disciplines. Due to the rate of change in every facet of personal and organizational life, this responsibility has to shift downward to include *all* managers and supervisors.

ORGANIZATIONAL LEARNING

Another application of the Ongoing Planning Database is in the area of organizational learning. One of the challenges of a growing category of organizational types—where employees work remotely from home or satellite offices—is the need to enhance productivity by streamlining communications as well as workflow systems and procedures.

For example, when a subsidiary or branch in one area of the country encounters a situation that triggers a Problem-Solving Session and a resolution is subsequently found, the details of that problem and its resolution should be available to all as a learning resource in the database. Thus, if another business unit encounters the same problem, it can access the database and discover a resolution without undergoing the same time-consuming and sometimes expensive Problem-Solving effort that the first business unit experienced.

A STRATEGIC MINDSET

At the end of a typical day, depending upon how many work sessions you've conducted or participated in, you could end up with several Action Plans. Some of these will likely indicate tasks and projects for which you are responsible.

Traditionally, managers with a challenging number of projects in various stages of completion rely upon a calendar-oriented to-do list of some sort. Since we've already alluded to the limitations of that approach, let's look at the elements that constitute a strategic mindset. In doing so, you'll see how the Personal Workflow Planner upgrades workflow management capabilities.

As shown in Figure 5.2, developing a strategic mindset requires the consideration of seven workflow management activity clusters. These are presented in circular format to make the point that strategy is an ongoing process, independent of conventional "start/stop" design limitations. For example, while "Issues" is the most logical starting point, every activity center is a potential Entry Point.

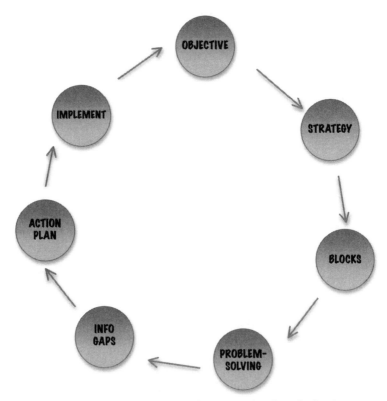

Figure 5.2   Activity clusters for a strategic mindset.

These workflow management activity clusters can be best understood by reframing them in a question context:

Objective: The objective could also be a goal or an issue, or the like—it doesn't matter. What's important is the question behind the activity; in this case that question is *What needs to get done?*

Strategy: A strategy is simply your plan to get it done. The underlying question is *How am I going to get it done?*

Blocks: A block refers to an obstacle that's preventing you from resolving an issue or solving a problem right now. The underlying question is *What's in the way?*

Logically, if you can't solve the problem yourself, you'd schedule it for a Problem-Solving Session with your team. Blocks appear in an unlimited array of circumstances and conditions. Even an Information Gap can become a block if we can't get the information or data we need to move ahead with a minimal level of confidence.

Problem-Solving: Blocks that defy resolution are most often entered in the Problem-Solving column of our Workflow Planners. Sometimes, however, you'll go right to an Innovation Session—especially when the issue relates to a need for new products. As you will see, your Workflow Planner gives you five disposition options for any issue that needs to be resolved or problem that needs to be solved. The underlying question is *How do I want to get this issue resolved?*

111

Information Gaps: As we know, most Action Plans contain Information Gaps. Often, the timely resolution of a particular Information Gap prevents a much bigger problem from developing in the near or far term. The underlying question is *What don't I know that I'd like to know to proceed with more confidence?*

Action Plan: The Action Plan is the unifying factor in all aspects of workflow management, from collaboration sessions to Ongoing Planning. By providing transparency and accountability, Action Plans enable all managers to navigate change in a manner that maximizes success, minimizes failure, and takes advantage of opportunity. The underlying question is *Have I fully documented the investment of human and other capital in a manner that maximizes the viability of this project by all reasonable measures of value creation?*

Implementation: The implementation step should reflect a thorough commitment to success and a willingness to accept the responsibility for anything less. The underlying question is *Have I done my best and everything ethically possible to ensure success?*

The Workflow Planner is a tool that enables you to proactively manage these strategic imperatives—it's a tool you can customize to manage change in a manner compatible with your personal management style. (See Figure 5.3)

To conclude that Workflow Planners merely help managers get more done in a shorter period of time would be to

WORKFLOW PLANNER

TODAY'S DATE	ISSUE	NEXT STEPS	BLOCKS	PROBLEM-SOLVING	INNOVATION	INFORMATION GAPS	DUE DATE

Figure 5.3 The Personal Workflow Planner.

underestimate their benefits. Workflow Planners help managers to develop a more strategic perspective by prompting them to consider several disposition options for a given task.

For example, Veronica, the manager of a department, might be quite capable of completing a particular task herself. However, the long-term need to train and educate those reporting to her may trump the expediency factor in this instance. She may conclude that a Problem-Solving Session, led by a junior colleague (to free her to participate in content discussion), may be a more valuable option for the disposition of the task.

This is the thought process of a leader, a true creator of value for the organization. It is cultivated as a consequence of working with her Workflow Planner, which, by design, constantly reminds her of her workflow management options and prompts her to choose from the menu of five disposition options for every task or issue:

1. By the manager, in person (do it yourself)
2. By the manager, via delegation
3. In an Issues Management Session
4. In an Innovation Session
5. In a Problem-Solving Session

ZEN AND THE WORKFLOW PLANNER

Letting go of an ingrained habit that many of us share—the use of a calendar-oriented to-do list to manage personal

workflow tasks—can be a challenge. The freedom resulting from this unshackling, however, is worth the effort: It
enables us to manage issues from a reframed perspective,
one that focuses on what we *don't* know rather than seek-
ing confirmation of what's already known. Paradoxically,
one benefit of relinquishing the conventional mindset is an
improved ability to stay current with expanding workloads.

The nature of a manager's relationship to the unknown
is critical because change is the driving dynamic underlying
all issues that need to be managed, problems that require
solving, innovation that needs to occur, and planning that
must be relevant. The advantages of a mindset that focuses
on what is *not* known can be illustrated through an experience we've all shared: a new job.

Imagine yourself on your first day at a new job in a
new organization. Your new company makes widgets, and
your job is to be in charge of business development for this
major player in the widget industry. You've done your due
diligence, but since this is your first day on the job you now
have the opportunity to see what you've really gotten yourself into. Regardless of what you were told *before* you joined
the company, you are now in that pristine zone where your
only task is to discover the realities of your new job (what
you don't know).

Imagine how open you are in this type of situation—the
freshness of your curiosity. In Zen practice this is referred
to as "beginner's mind" or "empty mind"—a clearheaded
mindset that sparkles with curiosity and clarity of purpose.
A benefit of the Workflow Planner is that it frees you to
maintain an unprejudiced mindset as you manage issues,

solve problems, and cultivate an environment of innovative curiosity and intellectual courage for those reporting to you.

EFFECTIVE DECISION MAKING

Functionally, Workflow Planners constitute the collective linchpin of Ongoing Planning. They engender confidence in the decision-making process. This is because they provide you with the capability to choose from a range of strategically sound options, which helps you develop an ever-expanding sensitivity to interconnectivities and become more skillful in the art of reframing. Needless to say, when all managers develop these habits, the collective intellectual and creative capital of the organization is enriched.

For example, if a manager's day is filled to capacity with stuff that "just has to get done" and her boss drops an assignment on her that completely derails her well-laid plans for the day, a glance at her Workflow Planner will remind her of the go-to workflow management option—the Issues Management Session. In a twenty-minute Issues Management Session with her team, she can resolve several of the issues she was planning to handle alone and schedule the remaining issues for an Innovation or Problem-Solving Session.

On a more personal note, the Workflow Planner is a workflow application that enables all managers to do a better job of managing themselves because it provides the means to put themselves in a proactive (stress-free) mode.

CUSTOMIZE YOUR WORKFLOW PLANNER

Keep in mind that Workflow Planners are for your personal use to manage the issues that define the nature and scope of your responsibilities. The planners are a workflow management tool that helps you manage change in a manner compatible with your personal management style. You should feel free to customize the design of your Workflow Planner to suit your individual style. Just make sure your planner includes a visual reminder of your five task disposition options: do it yourself, delegate it, Issues Management Session, Innovation Session, and Problem-Solving Session.

A FINAL THOUGHT

Keep in mind that Personal Workflow Planners, as described thus far, are documents for personal use that are *not* submitted to the Planning Database. Be assured that there will be some temptation to interface the Personal Workflow Planners with the Planning Database. However, the trade-off of converting them from a personal planning tool to a Planning Database satellite application is significant and should be considered with caution. You'll find that once managers are using the Workflow Planners effectively, they'll be reluctant to give them up. For that reason, I suggest that the Personal Workflow Planners be installed as stand-alone personal work management tools.

Chapter 6

ONE-ON-ONE SESSIONS

While the cornerstone workflow management sessions we're discussing are utilized primarily for team collaboration, they can also be used to upgrade the effectiveness of one-on-one collaboration. This chapter introduces one-on-one sessions to manage issues, innovate, and solve problems with one other person, as an alternative to group or solo workflow management sessions. (We refer to this session as a one-on-one event, but it works just as well with three people.)

One-on-one collaboration is the established approach for activities such as performance feedback and compensation discussions. However, it can also be quite effective as an alternative to meetings for many workflow management tasks. One-on-one workflow management sessions have been underutilized because of the lack of structured sessions that would ensure productivity. As a consequence, time, talent, and opportunity are routinely wasted behind closed doors and a significant amount of group collaboration is scheduled as a knee-jerk alternative.

In this chapter, we'll discuss one-on-one collaborative sessions for Issues Management, Innovation, and Problem-Solving.

SWITCHING ROLES

The one-on-one collaboration sessions you are introduced to here are designed such that one person is the facilitator and the other is the participant; then the roles are switched. The changeover is an option, however, rather than a requirement; the same individual can facilitate the entire session. There are many reasons to choose this option, the two most common being when the session's purpose is accomplished with just a single round of facilitation and time constraints.

THE ONE-ON-ONE ISSUES MANAGEMENT SESSION

A one-on-one session can be utilized to resolve a large number of issues expeditiously with another individual. It can be conducted on the spur of the moment, and the human capital investment is minimal. The process can be as effective digitally as in person, and it can serve as a means to introduce another person to the Issues Management Session.

For purposes of simplicity, let's assume you're conducting an in-person, one-on-one Issues Management Session and that this is the first exposure to the process for your colleague. Your goal is twofold: (1) to resolve the issues at hand and (2) to introduce your colleague to the session. Let's further assume that you have scheduled one hour for this session.

If possible, have an easel with paper pads and colored markers available in the space where the one-on-one will be conducted. This is standard equipment among managers who utilize workflow management sessions.

A group Issues Management Session is the workflow session to use when there are many issues to be resolved and input from a group is desired, but the one-on-one version is ideal in instances where you determine that your desired outcome can be accomplished with just two people. This type of session is similar to the group Issues Management Session but is faster to execute because fewer people are involved.

FACILITATING A ONE-ON-ONE

I recommend that you experience running an Issues Management Session with a group before running a one-on-one version. However, if you decide otherwise, be aware that the basics of session facilitation don't change as a result of the number of people involved. My concern stems from the fact that the intimacy of the one-on-one setting feeds the natural impulse to get involved in content, to flit in and out of the facilitator role when it's just you and one other person. So it's incumbent upon you to remain steadfast in your role and to stay tightly

---

focused. Not only are you the host of the session, but you have a responsibility to do a good job of introducing your colleague to this type of workflow management session.

The fact that you're devoting all of your time to the task of facilitating with just one other individual might, at first glance, seem to be a waste of half of the human creativity and knowledge available. Be assured that it's not. If you adhere to the session process, the facilitation you are providing will leverage your colleague's cognitive capability to an extent that more than compensates for your lack of involvement in content.

Also, keep in mind that you and your colleague are going to switch roles at the end of the first half of the session. This introduces an additional responsibility for you to be aware of: In addition to facilitating the session yourself, you're teaching your colleague how to facilitate an Issues Management Session. To maximize the productivity of this activity, take notes as you facilitate. (This is something you should not do while facilitating a group Issues Management Session.)

Getting Started

Since this is the first workflow session for your colleague, you should start the session by explaining the difference between content and process and make certain he or she understands the importance of keeping them separate. Also explain the difference between conventional meetings and workflow management sessions. Basically, put the same amount of energy into prepping your colleague for the one-on-one session that you would put into preparing participants for a group Issues Management Session.

Write the heading "Information Gaps" on one of the easels and explain to your colleague what they represent and their importance to any workflow management session. Let your colleague know you're going to visually record all of the unanswered questions that come up during the session.

Next, write the heading "Issues" at the top of a second large sheet of paper and request that your colleague also write this on his or her notepad. Then instruct your associate as follows:

> Please write as many issues as possible that you think need to be addressed at this session. Start with issues that fall within your area of responsibility and then expand your list without restriction.
>
> Feel free to expand your perspective to include issues that are normally outside your area of responsibility. Please write quickly and be prepared to read your list to me so that I can display your issues on the easel. At this point of the session the emphasis is on quantity of issues, so you don't need to give a lot of thought to what you write. Just write as many issues as you can in the five minutes allotted for this.

Speed is an important factor in all workflow management sessions—even solo and one-on-one sessions. Your instructions should be to the point and crisp. Stay on purpose, and move things along at a pace that's challenging for your colleague.

Displaying

At the end of the five-minute period, instruct your colleague to stop writing and read aloud the list of issues. Record the issues on the easel as quickly as possible, and mount the paper sheets on the walls.

Identify Critical Issues

The next task is to identify those issues on the list that are critical. Instruct your colleague as follows:

> Please take five minutes to identify the issues that you think are most critical.

Display the critical issues on your easel, and assign a number to each issue. Then ask your associate to rank the issues in order of importance. Use a brightly colored marker to indicate the ranking.

Question Exercise

Every workflow management session should include the Question Exercise. In Problem-Solving Sessions, this exercise is used quite often because it's a means to expand the operating contexts of participants and it enables a reframing of the problem(s) being addressed. In an Issues Management Session, it is used less frequently. In all cases, however, it should play some role in the process you're executing. Conduct at least one question cycle with your partner, and board the questions.

Action Plan

Create a new page with the title "Action Plan." Ask your colleague:

> Can Critical Issue number one be resolved right now
> without a Problem-Solving Session? Please take up
> to three minutes to decide.

Your objective is to quickly determine whether Critical Issue #1 can be resolved without a Problem-Solving Session. Be careful: It's easy to lose your concentration during this phase and get involved in a discussion, especially when it's just you and one other person. Your objective is to focus on time (process), not on the subject being discussed (content). Do not allow this phase to exceed three minutes.

Some of the critical issues on the list may be resolvable quite quickly. Others will be more complicated and defy resolution in the one-on-one Issues Management Session. These will be tagged for a later Problem-Solving Session. Feel free to mention the availability of the Problem-Solving alternative for those issues that cannot be immediately resolved, but do *not* get involved in any content discussion until the session is over.

Let's assume your associate thinks Critical Issue #1 doesn't require a Problem-Solving Session—maybe it's an issue that simply needs the timely and coordinated attention of a few people to prevent it from becoming a more serious problem. In that case, since formalized Problem-Solving is not required, resolve Critical Issue #1 as quickly as possible and promote it to Action Plan status.

Like Information Gaps, the Action Plan is a staple of all workflow management sessions, and all workflow sessions conclude with one for purposes of productivity, transparency, and accountability.

Once an issue has been resolved in a one-on-one Issues Management Session, or in any of the workflow management sessions, it's promoted to the Tasks/Next Steps column of the Action Plan.

When an issue has been resolved, your associate needs to either agree to complete the task or delegate someone else to do so. The name of the responsible party is recorded in the "Responsibility" column.

Any Task/Next Step that is agreed upon and for which an individual has been assigned responsibility must also have a Due Date assigned. Without a deadline, the integrity of any work session is questionable. Due Dates are important to create ownership and acknowledge the interconnectivity of all tasks, projects, and initiatives in an organization.

The "Report" column identifies the individual(s) to whom task results will be submitted. In one-on-one sessions, this can be discussed and agreed upon.

Return to Critical Issues

Now address Critical Issue #2, and repeat the same process. Let's assume that your associate is unable to resolve the next critical issue in the time allocated. Simply tag it for resolution via a Problem-Solving Session to be conducted after the one-on-one session is complete, or schedule it for a later time.

Record the Critical Issue on the Action Plan with the appropriate entries in each column. Continue this procedure with the remaining Critical Issues, recording the disposition of each either through immediate resolution or via a later Problem-Solving Session.

CONDUCT A POSTSESSION DISCUSSION

From many perspectives, the postsession discussions can be quite productive. As a teaching and learning opportunity, you can expedite your colleague's learning curve with this protocol and refine your personal workflow management session skills. To help jump-start that process, here are some issues you might want to address:

- What questions do you have about the session?
- What did you learn about your own workflow management session capabilities?
- What did you have most difficulty with?
- Are you clear about your Next Steps?
- How could I have done a better job as facilitator?
- How could you have done a better job?

Switch Roles

Assuming your colleague is up for it, and time permitting, switch roles and allow the other person to facilitate a one-on-one Issues Management Session with you as participant. Focus on doing a good job in the role. Stay in character, and don't offer any commentary on your colleague's facilitation performance until the postsession discussion for this one-on-one session. There is, however, one exception: Because it's your colleague's first time facilitating, remind him or her, when necessary, to focus exclusively on process and to ignore content.

THE ONE-ON-ONE INNOVATION SESSION

Usually, you get the most out of an Innovation Session when it's done with a group. However, there are times when you want to simply explore some possibilities with a colleague informally. This can be for purposes of reviewing business development possibilities, streamlining communications, uncovering preemptive positioning strategies for your brand, or introducing an associate to the innovation process. Whatever the reason, the Innovation Session is not restricted to formalized group settings. A one-on-one session is capable of delivering outcomes as diverse as a solution to a systemic research and development problem or uncovering a billion-dollar new product concept.

Although all of these issues would probably benefit more from a full-blown group Innovation Session, the value and economies of one-on-one and solo innovation efforts should never be underestimated.

The one-on-one Innovation Session is designed to provide the means for two people to assist each other to access their respective creative potentials for a specific purpose. Let's assume this is an in-person (see box) collaboration, your colleague is unfamiliar with the session, and you've allocated one hour for the session.

IN-PERSON VS. DIGITAL SESSIONS?

Yes, you can conduct one-on-one Innovation Sessions digitally, but it's best to have the experience of conducting an in-person session beforehand. This applies to all of the workflow management sessions we discuss—learn how to do them in person before you do them digitally.

Facilitating

Since this is the first workflow management session for your partner, start the session by explaining what the role of facilitator entails and the difference between content and process. You need to ensure your colleague's success by conveying a clear understanding of the dynamics that differentiate workflow management sessions from conventional meetings.

Speed

Speed plays an important role in all workflow management sessions because a fast pace generates a high level of energy. This is especially important in a one-on-one Innovation

Session, so set a brisk pace for yourself and your partner. While conducting this session, keep in mind that, for your purposes, imagination is more important than knowledge.

Innovation Session Phases

All Innovation Sessions (group, one-on-one, and solo) are composed of four phases: *Ideation, Building, Evaluation,* and *Action Plan.* The key to a successful Innovation Session of any type is to make sure the Ideation and Building phases are kept separate from the Evaluation phase.

Phase One: Ideation

It's as important to get agreement on the purpose of a one-on-one workflow management session as it is with a group collaborative session. Again, the core dynamics of workflow management sessions don't change much among solo, one-on-one, and group versions.

After a brief discussion with your associate, write up what you understand to be the goal of the session—for example: "To discover preemptive brand positioning possibilities." Mount this page on a wall or an easel. Then ask your partner to write the heading "Ideas" at the top of a page, and you do likewise on an easel.

Information Gaps
Since all workflow management sessions include the identification of Information Gaps, begin this one-on-one Innovation Session by writing "Information Gaps" on an easel.

Empty Mind

Just about everyone comes into an Innovation Session with some ideas they've already thought about. Your first step is to get these ideas down on paper so your partner can participate free of preconceived ideas. Instruct your partner as follows:

> Please take five minutes to write down any ideas you already have about a new brand positioning.

Let the person know when thirty seconds are left.

Displaying

Ask your colleague to articulate his or her ideas. Record them on your easel, without making any comment about what you are recording other than to get clarification and agreement that you have accurately recorded the ideas.

Question Exercise

Without pausing, instruct your partner as follows:

> What questions should we ask at this point? Please write as many questions as you can think of. You may want to refer to the ideas we've just boarded. You have five minutes to do this. Please start.

Let your colleague know when thirty seconds remain. At the end of the five minutes, ask the person to stop but don't board the questions. Instead, without discussion, repeat the procedure, instructing your colleague as follows:

Now, take just one minute and ask a better question. Please start.

Displaying

At the end of the allotted time, ask your colleage to stop, and board the questions that have been produced.

Ideation

Again without pausing, give your colleague the following instruction:

> Please take five minutes and, using the questions on the walls as stimuli, write as many new brand positioning ideas or partial ideas as you can. Go for quantity; forget quality. Do not evaluate or self-censor. The sky is the limit here. This is your opportunity to get paid for being absurd. You have five minutes. Please start.

Age Exercise

Now, without pausing, give your colleague this directive:

> Imagine you have the choice to live for another five hundred years, at any age you wish. What age would you choose? Why? What would you do with that time? You have five minutes for this exercise. Please start.

Ideation

Let your colleague know when there are just thirty seconds left. At the end of the five minutes, ask the person to read his or her notes but do not record them. Instead, without discussion, give the following instruction:

> In the next five minutes, imagine as many new positioning ideas for the brand as possible. They need not be realistic. Please start.

Give the warning when there are just thirty seconds to go. At the end of five minutes, instruct your colleague to stop and read the new ideas for repositioning the brand, then display them.

KNOW WHEN TO STOP

In a one-on-one session of any type, always be sensitive to your partner's need for occasional breaks. For example, it might be a good time for a break following this last Ideation phase. Also, if you've scheduled only one hour for this session, you should always be aware of the time. If you have used up forty minutes already, you should now shift gears and go into the Building and Evaluation phases of the session. Remember that you also need to create an Action Plan before the elapsed time exceeds one hour.)

Question Exercise

If your energy levels are holding up and you think another round of Ideation might be productive, proceed with the session by instructing your colleague as follows:

Take a clean sheet of paper and, using everything that is on display—ideas, half-ideas, questions, and Information Gaps—as stimuli, query yourself, "What question needs to be asked at this point?" You have three minutes for this. Please start.

Ideation

At the end of the three minutes, ask your colleague to articulate his or her questions. Board them, and without further discussion give the following instruction:

Please take another three minutes and write as many new brand positioning ideas as possible. They need not be realistic. Please start.

Alert the person when there are thirty seconds left. At the end of the three minutes, ask your colleague to stop and board the ideas.

Phase Two: Building

Now you'll assist your colleague to build on the ideas that have already been boarded. You want your colleague to stay in the Ideation mode for this step and resist the temptation of evaluating the ideas that are generated. Instead, ask your colleague to look for possible idea combinations, patterns, and interconnectivities. Allot five minutes to do this, and then board the new ideas, using colors to highlight possible combinations and interconnectivities.

Phase Three: Evaluation

The Evaluation phase of a one-on-one Innovation Session is similar to the same phase in the group version. Two things need to happen:

1. Assist your colleague to convert the new *ideas* into new *concepts*, where possible; then only if he or she is *not* going to facilitate a round of innovation:

2. Together, make a judgment call about the viability of the top new product concepts. If your colleague is going to facilitate the next round, postpone Evaluation until both of you have had a chance to ideate. (For more information on the differences between new product ideas and new product concepts, see Chapter 3, "The Innovation Session.")

Ranking

While this step is action-filled in the typical group Innovation Session, in the one-on-one version it's relatively low-key. If your colleague has generated a lot of brand repositioning alternatives, it might be useful to number each one for reference purposes. Ranking provides a choice of Entry Points for subsequent reevaluation. With the exception of an Action Plan, this completes one cycle of the one-on-one Ideation session.

Phase Four: Action Plan

Like Information Gaps, the Action Plan is another staple of workflow management sessions. It's created at the conclusion of each workflow management session to provide transparency and accountability for the investment of human capital.

Switch Roles

As in all one-on-one sessions, you'll switch roles with your colleague after you finish your turn at facilitating. Sometimes, however, it makes sense to conduct the postsession discussion before the switch, while both of you still have things fresh in your minds. Your colleague may have many questions about the facilitator's role. Personally, I like to give and receive feedback midsession, before we switch roles.

Regardless of when you switch, be the best possible participant when it's your colleague's turn to facilitate. As with the one-on-one Issues Management and Problem-Solving sessions, stay in character as a session participant and don't offer any commentary on your colleague's performance until the postsession discussion. The only exception to this rule is if your partner ventures into content. Be patient—it's difficult for many people to shed a lifetime of conventional meeting habits and retrain themselves to focus on process exclusively.

THE ONE-ON-ONE PROBLEM-SOLVING SESSION

The one-on-one Problem-Solving Session is a work management session that two people can utilize to solve problems effectively. While it's not expected to produce the large-caliber results of a formalized group Problem-Solving Session, it can be relied upon to deliver solutions on a sustained basis with an economy of human capital, and it will produce better results than conventional Problem-Solving efforts. It also provides an alternative to the knee-jerk: "let's have a meeting" (and spend several thousands of dollars) mentality prevalent in most organizations.

Like all of the workflow management sessions we discuss, the one-on-one Problem-Solving Session is designed to accommodate the fast pace and interconnectivities of digital age organizational management. The sessions can be spontaneous or scheduled, and they can be completed in as little as twenty minutes, depending upon the number and complexity of problems that need to be addressed. Like all of the one-on-one sessions, the one-on-one Problem-Solving Session is as effective digitally as it is in the flesh.

For our purpose, let's assume you're conducting an in-person, one-on-one Problem-Solving Session with an associate and that this is his or her first exposure to the session. That makes your goal twofold: to assist the associate to solve the problem(s) and to introduce him or her to the one-on-one Problem-Solving process.

ON-THE-SPOT PROBLEM-SOLVING

While the group Problem-Solving Session is the basic work management session to be used when you have complex problems to be resolved and input from several individuals is desired, the one-on-one version is ideal for on-the-spot Problem-Solving. If the problem proves to be tougher than either of you imagined and

> resists resolution via the one-on-one approach, you have recourse with a group session.

Facilitating

As host of the one-on-one Problem-Solving Session, you'll play the role of facilitator for the first phase of the session with your colleague. As in the one-on-one Issues Management Session, you'll have a postsession discussion with your colleague to share your observations, make suggestions, and answer any questions.

Sometimes, colleagues simply need some fine-tuning of their facilitation skills to be ready to run group sessions. In all one-on-one sessions, it's a good idea to take notes to enhance the quality of your performance feedback at the end of the session, when there is an opportunity for you to share your observations and make suggestions before you switch roles. As mentioned, in addition to facilitating the session, you're teaching your colleague how to facilitate group one-on-one Problem-Solving. Keep in mind, however, what was mentioned earlier with regard to the suggested session learning sequence; it's best to tackle Issues Management first, then Innovation, and the Problem-Solving Session last.

Getting Started

Write the heading "Information Gaps" at the top on one of the easels, and explain to your colleague what these gaps are and their role in the Problem-Solving process. Explain why we visually record all of the unanswered questions that come up during the session and why what we *don't* know is at least as important as what we do know.

Process and Content

When introducing any of these workflow management sessions to someone, it's important to explain the difference between *content* and *process*. Bear in mind that this is the core dynamic of all the collaborative workflow management sessions we discuss. Also clarify the difference between conventional meetings and workflow management sessions.

Entry Points

By now you understand that the group Problem-Solving Session is an innovation-driven process; we don't try to cognitively hammer out solutions. Instead, we create an environment that entices the solution to reveal itself. The same is true for the one-on-one version. Begin by establishing agreement about the general nature and scope of the first problem to be addressed. Make sure you have a good understanding of the problem, and then address the task of identifying the best Entry Point to solve that problem.

Pattern Recognition

When conducting a Problem-Solving Session with several problems on the agenda, your first step should be to board all of the problems on separate sheets and instruct your associate to scan for possible patterns, as follows:

> Please review the problems displayed on the wall and identify any patterns you see that run through some or all of the problems. In other words, is there a common thread among them?

Often, you'll be able to reduce the number of problems by combining and editing them.

Clarify the Problem

For purposes of example, let's assume you have just one problem that needs to be addressed. On an easel, write a brief statement of the problem, as you understand it. Make this statement as simple as possible. Confirm that your associate agrees with your understanding of the problem. Edit as necessary until the problem statement satisfies your colleague. Let's assume you are in general agreement that this is the problem statement:

> Our competitors are recruiting so many of our top managers. What can we do to stop this?

Verify or Reframe the Problem

Now ask your colleague to take five minutes to write as many different interpretations of this problem as possible. Instruct the person to reframe each statement into a question using the phrase "What if" or "Could we," and encourage him or her to be as unrealistic, ridiculous, and absurd as possible. Give some examples of what you're looking for: "What if our managers couldn't leave us and go to work for the competition?" or "What if our managers had a reason to never want to leave?" or "What if we make it very difficult for our competitors to poach our managers?" or "Could we make it so our competitors never want to hire our people?"

Once your partner understands what you have in mind, give the person five minutes to write as many of these reframed questions as possible. Alert the person at thirty seconds before the time limit. As in a group session, this introduces the element of speed to the session and adds to the energy level (see box "Don't Dawdle").

At the end of the five minutes, instruct your associate to stop and read the reframed questions aloud so you can write them on your easel and then mount them. Confirm that your colleague is still satisfied with the original wording of the problem. If not, edit the statement of the problem as needed.

Sometimes reframing the problem reveals a solution or partial solution. Continually check whether your associate sees a solution, a partial solution, or even a hint of a solution among the reframed suggestions. If so, circle it with a brightly colored marker and continue the session.

DON'T DAWDLE

Your instructions in a one-on-one session should be as precise and crisp as if you were leading a fifteen-person group Problem-

---

Solving Session. Stay on-purpose and move things along at a challenging pace. Remember, the dynamics of the facilitator role are consistent, regardless of the type of work session you're conducting.

Solution Identified

If a solution is identified and your colleague is satisfied, write up the solution and proceed to the Action Plan phase. Then end the session.

If a solution is not identified, continue to the Question Exercise.

Question Exercise

Give your colleague the following instruction:

What questions need to be asked right now? Write down as many questions as you can think of within a three-minute period.

Let your colleague know when thirty seconds are left. Without pausing to record the questions, repeat the exercise at least two more times. After each cycle, repeat the instruction "Ask a better question."

At the end of three rounds, board and mount all questions.

Check for Solutions

When reviewing the questions produced by this exercise, it's a good idea to scan them for any patterns, similarities, or interconnectivities. It's possible your associate has the solution or part of the solution to the problem or that the solution is already mounted on the wall in the form of a question. So you need to check out this possibility by asking your colleague:

> Do you think that we have the solution or that we're close to a solution? Please scan everything mounted on the walls. Do you see a solution, or part of a solution, or a pattern that implies a solution?

Allow time for the person to offer solutions or partial solutions and to pose any questions that need to be answered. Sometimes, a previously unrecognized systemic problem is uncovered this way.

Make sure all of the questions that cannot be answered at this time are recorded on the Information Gaps sheet. Do not engage in any content discussion. There will be time for that at the end of the session. Keep the session moving at a smart pace.

Solution Identified

If a solution to the problem in question has been found, proceed to the Action Plan and then end the session.

If a solution has not been found, continue with the session.

Invisibility Exercise

Both group and one-on-one Problem-Solving Sessions utilize Ideation exercises. The key to successful Problem-Solving lies in achieving a balance between cognition (depending on rational, logical thinking) and creativity (see Chapter 4, "The Problem-Solving Session"). If you lose that balance, the cognitive dynamic always dominates and smothers creativity, a common occurrence in conventional meetings and brainstorming sessions (see Chapter 3, "The Innovation Session").

This is one of the reasons we insist upon the separation of content and process in all workflow sessions—to provide just enough structure and tension to achieve a spicy interaction between innovation and cognition.

Another reason is that it's especially important that you conduct a one-on-one Problem-Solving Session with the same commitment to enforcing the separation of Ideation and Evaluation that you would with a large group.

Here's an interesting Ideation exercise to run. Instruct your colleague as follows:

If you suddenly discovered that you had the ability to become invisible at will and walk through walls, steel, rock, and any other solid, and you were the only person who knew about this, how would it change your life? Please write your answer in as

144

much detail as possible. You have five minutes to complete this. Please start.

Ideation

Let your associate know when thirty seconds are left in the Invisibility Exercise. At the end of the five minutes, ask your colleague to articulate his or her answer. Do not write up the answers, and give no reaction to anything your colleague says. Instead, without pausing, give the following instruction:

> Please take a clean sheet of paper and write down five possible answers to the question "How can we stop competitors from hiring so many of our top managers?" You have five minutes to complete this exercise. Please start.

Let your colleague know when thirty seconds are left. At the end of the time, ask your colleague to stop, then board the proposed solutions, partial solutions, ideas, and so on. Also record any Information Gaps.

Depending upon the time available and the energy level of your associate, you may want to run another Ideation exercise using a different stimulus question. An example of another question to ask is:

> If you could hear sounds from any distance at will, just by focusing on the location, and no one knew about this, how would that change your life?

Check for Solutions

At the conclusion of every Ideation exercise in any Problem-Solving Session, one-on-one or group, immediately ask for more potential solutions to the problem. The Ideation exercises trigger the imagination and enable people to get outside their everyday Problem-Solving comfort zones; these exercises create openings through which people can see possibilities from a fresh perspective. You need to capitalize on these openings as fast as possible because most people quickly revert to their default rational mindset.

Solution Identified

When all of the possible solutions are boarded, ask your associate if he or she has identified the solution to the problem. If so, help to get it down on paper and then board it.

Once a solution for any problem has been identified, it should be promoted to an Action Plan. Your associate should either agree to complete the follow-up tasks or delegate someone else to do so. Record the name of the responsible party in the "Responsibility" column of the Action Plan.

End the session.

In many one-on-one sessions, a solution to the problem has been discovered by the time you reach this stage. If this is not the case, it's time to switch roles.

Switch Roles

Participants in one-on-one sessions switch roles after the first person finishes facilitating the session. In some situations, however, it makes sense to conduct the postsession discussion before the switch, while both of you still have things fresh in your minds. This is a judgment call for you to make. Again, I like to give and receive feedback midsession, before we switch roles.

Regardless of when you switch, give your all to be the best possible participant so that your colleague has a successful facilitation experience. As with the one-on-one Issues Management Session, stay in character as a session participant and do *not* offer any commentary on your colleague's facilitation performance until the one-on-one postsession discussion, unless your colleague ventures into the content area. Be patient—it is very difficult to focus on process exclusively and stay out of content.

Postsession Discussion

The postsession discussion can be quite productive in a one-on-one Problem-Solving Session. Since you are no longer in your role of facilitator, you'll have the opportunity to offer your suggestions and insights. If necessary, you and your colleague can work through a Building phase and then an Evaluation phase as part of the postsession discussion. This can be valuable for both of you, especially if a solution to the problem was not discovered.

In many cases, however, the solution, or at least a partial solution, has surfaced through this process. When your input is added to the session outcome, a better or alternative resolution might be uncovered.

In any event, as with the Issues Management and Innovation one-on-one sessions, you'll have some thoughts to share with your associate once the session is completed. To help jump-start that process, ask the same follow-up questions as you did after the other sessions:

- What questions do you have about the one-on-one session?
- What did you learn about your personal capabilities [in this case, for Problem-Solving]?
- What part of the process did you have the most difficulty with?
- What part of the process were you most comfortable with?
- Are you clear about your Next Steps?
- How could I have done a better job as facilitator?
- How could you have done a better job?

Chapter 7

SOLO SESSIONS

Mostly, managers perform in one of three venues: their personal office, a conference room, or a boss's office. All three are used for meetings. A small portion of managers' time is spent alone in their own offices. That's the area of focus for this chapter.

My purpose is to introduce three self-management tools to enable those who lead others to maximize their own productivity *between* collaborative sessions. These three tools, which help you be more productive during your solo time in the workplace, are individualized versions of the group Issues Management, Innovation, and Problem-Solving sessions.

To run a productive solo workflow management session, you must be able to separate process from content without the benefit of a facilitator and be capable of switching back and forth in the alternate roles of facilitator and participant, without getting lost in content. This means you adopt the role of a *bridger*, one who can do both. (This is one of the reasons that I strongly recommend you acquire experience in facilitating group workflow sessions before you make use of their corresponding solo versions.)

SOLO SESSIONS AND THE PERSONAL WORKFLOW PLANNER

Resist the temptation to resort to a to-do list when you run your first solo Issues Management Session. Instead, use the opportunity to create a Personal Workflow Planner (see Chapter 5, "The Ongoing Planning Process"). This is a critical-path workflow management tool that you'll use to stay current with robust workloads of any complexity. Your Workflow Planner includes tasks and responsibilities that can be done alone, some that require collaboration, and many that warrant both individualized and collaborative attention. Time and personnel are best utilized, and productivity maximized, when the appropriate balance of all three work session types (solo, one-on-one, and group) is achieved. The solo Issues Management process helps you achieve this balance.

THE SOLO ISSUES MANAGEMENT SESSION

While the group Issues Management Session is the basic workflow management session for leveraging intellectual and creative capital, this session type is also a powerful resource when you are faced with a workload that you want to assess personally to determine whether you need or desire group input. The solo Issues Management process enables you to quickly identify all Critical Issues, resolve those that you can, and be certain about which issues would best benefit from delegation or collaborative attention.

This session helps you to get a fix on how you want to handle day-to-day issues *before* you collaborate with others. Properly executed, this not only enables you to get more done in a fraction of the time it would normally require but also ensures that the expense of group collaboration, when utilized, is justified. There is no better way to prepare for a productive group Issues Management Session, and this solo session facilitates a judicious allocation of time and personnel.

Any issues you are unable to resolve or choose not to address are scheduled for handling in a subsequent collaborative workflow session. This usually is an Issues Management Session or a Problem-Solving Session. However, it could also be a one-on-one.

Action Plans are not used in solo sessions, and outcomes are not submitted to the Ongoing Planning Database.

Getting Started

On a digital device, create a file titled "Issues" and add today's date. Next, list all of the issues you want to resolve, regardless of how big, small, complex, or vague they might be. The key to a successful solo workflow session is to resist the natural inclination to prioritize or assign any type of classification to the issues at this stage. Discipline yourself to withhold evaluation, analysis, and judgment while you're executing this first step—just get all the issues out of your head and onto your screen in whatever order they occur to you.

Now go through your list and put an asterisk in front of any issue you consider to be critical. A Critical Issue is one that needs immediate attention: a problem that needs to be solved right away, information that needs to be communicated to those who report to you, a trend that needs immediate attention before it becomes irresolvable, a request from your superior about a personnel issue, critical Information Gaps you need to get answered, competitive information that needs assessment, and the like.

Workflow Framing

Once you've created a list of the Critical Issues, rank them according to how quickly they need to be resolved. Address Critical Issue #1 and decide whether you can resolve it yourself. If you can resolve it, do so. If you cannot or choose not to resolve that issue now, mark it for one of two Next Steps: (1) delegation to another person or (2) inclusion in a group or one-on-one Issues Management Session. This is an important step because you're about to frame all of the issues you don't or can't or choose not to resolve immediately in this manner.

Notice that your options did not include scheduling the issue for a group Problem-Solving or Innovation Session. All group collaboration sessions begin as Issues Management Sessions to maximize the likelihood of resolution within that session. In the event the issue is *not* resolved in the Issues Management Session, then you and your team can decide on the most appropriate Next Step: Innovation or Problem-Solving. This is a key aspect of effective solo workflow management: Things either get handled right now, are delegated, or are promoted to a group or one-on-one Issues Management Session. The process is simple and efficient.

Sometimes you'll want to submit an issue that you've already resolved to a group or one-on-one Issues Management Session. This is an effective way to confirm the integrity of your critical thinking with regard to the disposition of a particular issue. It's also a good jump-start vehicle for any collaborative work session.

In the event you do submit such an issue during a group Innovation Session that you're facilitating, let the participants know which issue you want to submit before you assume the role of facilitator. Ideally, you should have someone junior to you run that session.

Needless to say, you should not participate in any discussions about this issue if you're the one facilitating the session. Furthermore, once you submit any issues for group consideration, they become collaborative issues; outcomes relating to them are therefore recorded on the Action Plan and subsequently fed to the Planning Database and distributed to all participants (see Chapter 5, "The Ongoing Planning Process").

THE SOLO INNOVATION SESSION

Once you're familiar with the group Innovation Session, the solo version enables you to tap into your own creative potential between collaborative sessions. A significant benefit of this session is that it can be done on your schedule, in any location, and all you need is paper and pen. You can use your computer for solo innovation work, but when you do it for the first time I recommend that you use just pen and paper, which you can utilize without electricity (in the case of impromptu sketches, for example) in a variety of circumstances.

You can use the solo Innovation Session for an unlimited number of purposes:

- To upgrade systems and procedures
- To revitalize business development programs, to create new products and services
- To streamline communications
- And even to identify where innovative scrutiny is most needed within the organization

A safe bet is to assume that every system and procedure within the organization would benefit from an innovative upgrade. A solo Innovation Session can be completed in twenty minutes. After your first session, you'll be able to extract elements from the process (i.e., a particular Ideation exercise) and complete the session in a few minutes. For your first run, however, plan on a half hour, and try to ensure that there will be no interruptions.

Solo Innovation Sessions comprise three phases: *Ideation, Building,* and *Evaluation.* (This is the same structure as the collaborative version, but without the Action Plan element.) As in the collaborative version, the key to a successful solo Innovation Session is making sure the Ideation and Building phases are kept separate from the Evaluation phase. As you know, the reason for this is that Ideation and Building are creative activities, while Evaluation is a mostly cognitive process; if you combine them, the cognitive dynamic (*Evaluation*) dominates, and you end up with very few ideas (see Chapter 3, "The Innovation Session"). Separating the Ideation and Evaluation phases is not easy for most people. Nevertheless, it is an important issue in this process.

In group Innovation Sessions, the task of keeping the Ideation and Evaluation phases separate is handled by the facilitator. For that reason, I recommend that you facilitate an Innovation Session with a group before you run the solo version. It requires some practice to do it successfully on your own with consistency.

CHALLENGE YOURSELF

By imposing short completion cycles on yourself, you increase your energy level, short-circuit rational thought processes, and more easily access your creative capabilities. That's why speed plays such an important role in group workflow sessions. A fast pace keeps you actively involved and jars you out of your cognitive comfort zone. Keep that in mind while executing the solo Innovation Session.

Phase One: Ideation

When you run a solo Innovation Session, it's important that you keep a record of all the questions you come up with that you can't answer. Those questions you choose not to resolve yourself should be delegated for immediate resolution. As already mentioned, Information Gaps should not be allowed to accumulate (who knows what lurks therein?). Even in a solo Innovation Session, you should maintain a permanent display for Information Gaps. This is a further acknowledgment of the importance of the unknown in best practices to all of the workflow management.

Purpose of the Session

In a solo Innovation Session you need to be just as clear about what you want to achieve as you would in a group session. A good way to verify your purpose is to state it in as few words as possible, for example, "determine how to upgrade quality control systems and procedures." Write it down, then give yourself this challenge:

Can I improve upon this statement of purpose?

Remain open to the possibility that your statement can be improved upon or made more specific. Fine-tune your original as needed. Take no more than five minutes to complete this.

It's quite possible that you already have some ideas related to your statement of purpose. If so, you need to get those ideas out of your head and onto paper. This accomplishes two things:

1. It jump-starts the Ideation.
2. It clears your head of preconceived ideas. An empty mind is needed for productive Ideation.

Clear Your Mind

Write the heading "Ideas" on a sheet of paper, and then write down as many ideas for quality control system and procedure upgrades as you can. Many of these will be ideas you've been kicking around in your head for some time; others will be new ideas that occur to you in the course of this session. Simply write them all down as quickly as you can. Strive for quantity of ideas. Don't evaluate or censor yourself in any way. And enjoy the process. Having fun is a key ingredient in successful Ideation, so let your imagination run wild. Emphasize the outlandish, the improbable, and the impossible, as opposed to the logical and feasible. Forget viability for the moment, and strive for quantity of ideas. No one needs to see what you're writing. Give yourself five minutes for this task.

Ideation

At the end of five minutes, stop and, without breaking stride, give yourself the directive to write three additional ideas. (When I do this I imagine I have a personal facilitator who's guiding me.) Feel free to write partial ideas as well as complete ideas and even morsels of ideas; also build on the ideas you've already written down. But don't censor yourself or evaluate anything you write. Likewise, resist the urge to "fall in love with" any of your ideas at this point. Give yourself three minutes to complete this step.

Question Exercise

As you know by now, one of the most powerful drills you can run during any workflow management session is the

Question Exercise. In a group Innovation Session, this exercise is conducted a few times every hour. In a solo Innovation Session, you should use it just as frequently. Query yourself: "What question should I ask myself at this point?" Write as many questions as possible. Give yourself three minutes for this.

At the end of three minutes, stop and challenge yourself to ask one more question —a better one. As we've established, the main purpose of the Question Exercise is to expand your viewpoint and enable you to reframe issues in a manner that expands your operating context at will. But it can also be used to contract your viewpoint, which can be just as important. The ability to do both enhances your creative and cognitive capabilities.

Ideation

At the end of the three minutes, stop and make sure your list is legible. Then take a blank sheet of paper and, using your lists as stimuli, write as many ideas as possible. Write quickly. Again, quantity is the only requirement. Do not evaluate or censor or spend too much time on any one idea. There will be time for that later. Give yourself no more than three minutes for this.

When the three minutes are up, stop and review your list for legibility. Put your list aside and repeat this Ideation step. Challenge yourself to come up with at least five new ideas—with no evaluation. When the three minutes are up, stop.

Ideation Exercise

Now it's time to challenge your imagination in a more aggressive mode. For this exercise, you'll need paper and pen. If possible, use a large paper pad (easel size) and some colored markers. Proceed as follows: Off the top of your head and without deep thought, express three new ideas graphically. Don't use words; sketch the ideas. (Ignore the fact that you may consider yourself unable to draw.) Use the whole sheet of paper—the bigger the sketches, the better. Imagine the sketches to be the only way you have to communicate your ideas. Sketch as simply or as elaborately as you wish. Stretch yourself. Go outside of your comfort zone. Use bright colors if you have colored markers and bold strokes. No one needs to see these drawings. When you fill up a sheet of paper, get a fresh one. Give yourself five minutes to do this. It is very important that you do not evaluate your work.

At the end of the five minutes, write the ideas the sketches represent on your Ideas list. Do not evaluate them.

Follow this exercise with as many other Ideation exercises as you want, as long as they continue to be productive (see box "Access Your Own Creative Potential").

ACCESS YOUR OWN CREATIVE POTENTIAL

Chapter 3, "The Innovation Session" introduced a number of creativity exercises. Readers will find more of these in Chapter 8, "Making It Happen". These creativity exercises are essential for accessing new ideas and solutions in group workflow

---

management sessions. There is no reason not to use them in solo sessions as well.

For example, in addition to the Ideation (Sketch) Exercise described in this chapter, you can run another solo creativity exercise called Jobs. Simply imagine that you and everyone else on the planet must change jobs, and your new career must be in a completely different area. What job would you choose if your status, income, and so on, would remain exactly the same as it is right now? What would be your first choice for an alternative job? Take three minutes to list your top five choices.

Once your list is complete, immediately write three new ideas for upgrading systems and procedures. If this Jobs Exercise is producing ideas, regardless of how ridiculous, repeat it one more time and write any new ideas that occur to you . Remember, your goal is quantity of ideas, not quality. As previously, don't evaluate your work.

Phase Two: Building

At this point, you will have many ideas about how to upgrade quality control systems and procedures. Now it's time to do some Building. The key to having a successful Building phase is to concentrate on ways to make ideas work and avoid the natural tendency to focus on why something might not work. For this reason, Building is best done while you're still in the Ideation frame of mind.

Carefully review your list of ideas for interconnectivities, combinations, and patterns. Edit your work in a manner that clarifies each idea, and assign a number to each idea in preparation for the final step: Evaluation.

DON'T UNDERESTIMATE SOLO SESSIONS

The Building phase illustrates why group Innovation Sessions usually produce superior outcomes as compared to solo sessions. Groups produce the benefit of hundreds of ideas to work with as opposed to just your own output. However, keep in mind that no one knows where the next billion-dollar idea will come from. It could be on the page in front of you right now.

Phase Three: Evaluation

The purpose of the Evaluation phase in a solo Innovation Session is to enable you to make an informed judgment call about the viability of each new idea. Review each idea and assign it a viability value ranging from 1 to 3, with 3 indicating the highest level of viability.

Any ideas to which you assign a value of 3 are ideas that, in your opinion, are worthy of further consideration in the quest to upgrade quality control systems and procedures in your department. These are ideas you'd feel comfortable sharing with others for feedback and possible implementation.

Ideas scoring a 2 or a 1 are those you might be willing to share after some further thought and refinement. All of the ideas and concepts are allocated a file dedicated to Innovation Session outcomes, both solo and collaborative.

Before you end the session, remember to assign any Information Gaps for resolution and include them in your Personal Workflow Planner.

You may opt to run a group Innovation Session if you feel less than satisfied with your solo outcome. Many managers run a solo Innovation Session as a precursor to a group session. There are several advantages to this workflow strategy. For example, your ideas can be used to jump-start the group Ideation phase: The group gets the benefit of your content contribution, and it enables you to do a better job of facilitation because you can let go of the temptation to get involved in content.

Or, as previously suggested, arrange for the session to be facilitated by someone junior to you who's been trained in the workflow management process. That way you get to be a participant, and the group gets the benefit of your knowledge, experience, perspective, and creativity.

THE SOLO PROBLEM-SOLVING SESSION

Solo Problem-Solving can be an economically sound alternative to group sessions in some situations. Just because you have the ability to leverage the cognitive and creative capital of others to solve problems doesn't mean you should always opt to do so. Once you acquire the skill to facilitate workflow sessions, you can choose to resolve many problems independently. In this instance, assume a problem exists that you've decided to address personally, using the Solo Problem-Solving protocol.

Again, I strongly recommend that you facilitate each of the group collaboration sessions (Issues Management, Innovation, and Problem-Solving) before you utilize the solo Problem-Solving Session. The skills and exercises in each of the sessions are introduced sequentially and culminate with the Solo Problem-Solving process.

Entry Points

The selection of a strong (highly leveraged) Entry Point is critical in the solo Problem-Solving process because it enables you to identify solutions to problems faster than would a haphazard selection. Asking the right question at the start of the process aims you in the right direction, saving time and effort. Selecting an Entry Point that is highly leveraged gets you closer to the solution faster. (Refer back to Figure 1.2 for a visual representation of this.)

Information Gaps

Create a file titled "Information Gaps" in which to document any questions that occur to you that you can't answer during the session. The procedure for handling Information Gaps after a solo session is different from that following a group collaborative session. You don't conclude the solo session with an Action Plan; instead, you work with your Personal Workflow Planner (see Chapter 5, "The Ongoing Planning Process").

Record all Information Gaps in that file and take whatever steps are at your disposal to get the answers.

Question Exercise

In solo workflow sessions, the Question Exercise is a challenging process for many because of our reflexive reaction to attempt to answer any question we're asked, regardless of the quality or integrity of the question. In group Problem-Solving Sessions, the facilitator functions as a guide to make participants comfortable with the process of question discrimination, whereas in a solo session, you're on your own. Therefore, you need to undergo several rounds of the Question Exercise to make sure you're not satisfied too easily.

Getting Started

As with all sessions, begin the solo Problem-Solving Session by stating the problem, then ask yourself, "What question needs to be asked?" Write down your question(s), but do not attempt to answer any of them. Instead, challenge yourself to repeat the process and come up with a better question.

The problem we begin with often turns out to be the wrong problem. By focusing on the quality of the questions we're asking, however, we can discover the question that reveals the best Entry Point to use to get at the right problem. Rarely will this question reveal itself without some work.

Pattern Recognition

When you think you've exhausted your ability to ask any more questions, look at your list of questions and see if you can identify any patterns. Does any question grab your attention more than the others? Are there any interconnections between any of the questions? Is there a common thread that runs through some or all of the questions? Most important, is a solution to the problem suggested?

If the answer to the last question is "yes," make an entry in your Workflow Planner and end the session.

Do you have a different understanding of the problem than you started with? If yes, restate the problem on your screen and repeat the solo Problem-Solving process, starting with the Question Exercise.

What-If Exercise

Now reframe the problem in as many ways as you can, beginning each reframed question with "What if." Here are some examples:

- What if we took no action?
- What if the roles were reversed and the competition was addressing this problem—what would they do?
- What if we had unlimited resources to apply to this problem? What would we do first? What would we do after that?
- What if we had seen this problem coming or about to happen—what would we have done about it?
- What if we could wave a magic wand and postpone this problem for six months—what would we do today?

Solution Identified

When you have as many "What ifs" as you can think of in a five-minute period, review all of them for any patterns, repetitions, correlations, or interconnectivities. Then challenge yourself to quickly write at least five possible solutions to the problem within a three-minute time period.

Speed is important here, so focus on generating a large quantity of possible solutions. Don't evaluate; just enjoy the process. Allow your sense of the ridiculous to stimulate your imagination. Remember, no one needs to see the list you generate at this point.

Review your list of solutions. Is an answer to your problem suggested? If the answer is "yes," make an entry in your Workflow Planner, then end the session. Or select the next problem to be solved and run the session again.

If an answer has not revealed itself, you need to ask yourself the following question: Do I want to continue attempting to resolve this problem in the solo mode? If you choose to collaborate, you have two options: one-on-one collaboration with a colleague or a formalized Problem-Solving Session with other members of your team. You'll potentially benefit the most from a group session, but it's a bigger investment of human capital than the one-on-one or solo options.

If you opt for collaboration, clean up your Information Gaps document and your Solutions list, since you can use them to jump-start the collaborative Problem-Solving Session. Keep in mind that, when resolved, one of the Information Gaps may prove to be a treasure trove of solutions and/or partial solutions. For that reason, record them in your

Personal Workflow Planner and make sure they're addressed as soon as possible.

Ideation Exercise

If you elect to continue in the solo mode, it's time to change gears and tap into your imagination as a means to get an answer to the problem you've been dealing with. The exercise presented here helps you to get outside of your everyday Problem-Solving comfort zone and address the problems from a fresh perspective.

> Imagine that all of a sudden you knew the outcome of every game in every major professional sport, before it was played. What would you do about that? Take five minutes to list exactly what you would do.

At the end of the five minutes, list all possible solutions or questions that occur to you. Take no more than five minutes to do this. When the five minutes are up, stop and review your list of solutions. Is an appropriate solution to your problem suggested? If the answer is "yes," record it in your Personal Workflow Planner. End the session.

KNOW WHEN TO STOP

Based on my experience with solo Problem-Solving, I believe that you'll know relatively quickly if you're going to solve the

---

problem or not. Unlike a group setting, which generally uncovers many viable solutions to several problems in one session, the solo outcomes tend to be less dramatic than those produced by the corresponding group versions. That's one of the reasons I recommend a specific session learning sequence: group sessions first, one-on-ones next, and solo last.

For the group sessions, start with Issues Management, followed by Innovation and then Problem-Solving, in that order. The same learning sequence holds true for one-on-ones and solo. After some group experience, however, you'll find your one-on-ones and solo outcomes get better and better.

Chapter 8

MAKING IT HAPPEN

Ideation is a tool for accessing and leveraging the creative potential of individuals and groups. It's an integral part of all the workflow management sessions presented in this book. Most managers justify their lack of attention to this issue by citing demanding workloads of a more "pragmatic" nature. However, the pace of innovation set by the technological evolution puts enormous demands on leadership in other industries to stay relevant.

This chapter helps you to convert your organization to an innovative entity by bringing an innovative mindset to every aspect of workflow management. We'll accomplish this in three stages: first, some reminders about how to get the most out of the Innovation processes you've already learned; then, examples of Ideation exercises you can utilize in your organizations right now; and, finally, the secret for developing Ideation exercises customized to your own organization and industry.

REMINDERS

Lead by Example

It's up to you to set the tone for upbeat, enjoyable, and productive workflow sessions. You have a responsibility to lead by example, so don't bring any personal negativity to a work session. You need to show up looking well-rested and filled with positive energy. This attitude is contagious, so let the group see that you are enjoying yourself.

Validate

Expect to do a lot of encouraging and validating. Your role is to orchestrate a roomful of mainly pragmatic minds to switch mental gears and tap into their creative capabilities. For many people, this is a new and potentially exciting experience.

Expect Success

As a facilitator, you need to remember a very important fact: There is enough intellectual and creative talent in the conference room to solve any work-related problem and identify a billion-dollar idea. Your job is twofold: (1) to convince the participants of their unused creative potential and (2) to provide them with the environment and the collaborative tools to access it.

Always Be Asking

In sales, it's a well-known fact that the most success-ful salespeople don't hesitate to ask for the order; they're "always closing." Similarly, you should always be asking for new ideas. Don't get so wrapped up in the excitement of the session that you forget your purpose: to elicit innovative ideas and breakthrough solutions.

Handle the Chaos

A hardworking group often becomes so loud and excited that the session appears to be chaotic. Properly guided, the moment that seems most chaotic can also be the most pro-ductive point in the session. As you gain experience as a facilitator, you'll be able to create the right balance between chaos and structure. I achieve that balance by imagining myself located at the center of a cyclone. That way, I can "stir the pot" and not worry about losing control of the group. In short, the most productive Ideation sessions frequently flirt with what appears to be chaos. Because of the agreement you have with the group in all workflow sessions—that you're in charge of process—you can manage chaos to everyone's benefit.

Stay Tuned In

Always be tuned in to the energy level of your group and allow yourself to be influenced by them in terms of when to take breaks, which Ideation exercises to select, and how long sessions should last. You are there to enable the participants to exceed their normal collaborative performance. How you collaborate with them dictates how well they collaborate with each other.

Clarify Instructions

Continually ask the group whether there is anyone who does not understand an instruction before you direct them to begin a new process or cycle. If you don't, you're likely to experience interruptions midcycle by participants who are uncertain or confused. This slows down the pace of the session and deflates the energy in the room.

Maintain Speed

Speed plays an important role in all workflow management sessions because it creates the tendency to bypass rational thought; it doesn't give participants the time to settle into their cognitive comfort zones. So make your instructions to the group precise and to the point. Doing so short-circuits rational thought processes and, in their place, encourages uncensored creativity.

Refrain from Judging

Be extra firm about refraining from evaluation during an Ideation phase. By instructing a group to strive for quantity of ideas, you deny them the time to indulge in self-censorship and evaluation. This is tougher for them than it might appear: You're asking a group of individuals to stop something they've been conditioned to do all of their adult lives. Be patient with them.

Free Their Minds

Most participants in an Ideation exercise already have some ideas in mind before the start of the process. You need to get all of these ideas and opinions out of their heads and onto paper as quickly as possible. Otherwise, those ideas will prejudice and contaminate their contributions throughout the session.

Restrict Discussion

By restricting discussion during most sessions and exercises, you intensify individual focus, build the desire to collaborate, and minimize distractions. Make sure the group understands that there will be ample time allotted for discussion in every session.

Encourage Laughter

Laughter is an important ingredient in the innovative process. I encourage laughter and rarely miss an opportunity to make the group laugh. I laugh at myself a lot. It helps release pent-up stress and enables enjoyable creativity. In general, the more laughter there is in an Innovation Session, the better the results.

In ancient times, it was standard practice for abbots in monasteries of certain sects to instruct the monks to go into the forest at dawn and laugh. Today, science has confirmed the correlation between laughter and a chemical change that occurs in the brain. The nature of that change is an improvement in the person's feeling of well-being. In general, the more you laugh, the better you feel and function.

Maintain Control

Stay in control of the group. It's a big part of your job. You've probably noticed an apparent paradox here: You're imposing structure to enable the group to be creative. It works.

Know When to Wait

In horse racing, one of the skills that separate the great jockeys from the rest of the pack is their uncanny ability to know how long to wait for the other horses to tire before giving their mounts the signal to go flat-out. Cultivate that sense of oneness, sensitivity, and timing with your group. Know when to push for more creative effort and when to ease up and let the participants recoup their energy.

Aim for Fluidity

It's important to spend as little time as possible on the logistics of going from individual to team processes because you want to maintain the high energy level of the group. With practice, you'll be able to orchestrate the group to shift gears quickly and with fluidity.

Stand Up

Assuming you can, always conduct workflow management sessions on your feet. Motion generates energy. One of the hallmarks of the conventional meeting model is that everyone is sitting down. Some are asleep.

One of the many ways to keep a group involved is to conduct some exercises while participants are standing instead of sitting. Another interesting energy change-up is to give the group the option of sitting or standing for some or all of the work session.

Throw a Change-Up

We're all creatures of habit, and there's nothing wrong with that. Some interesting things result, however, when you instruct your session participants to execute any Ideation exercise with their opposite hand (i.e., those who are right-handed should write with their left hand, and vice versa). It's well worth trying this during your next Ideation exercise.

Show, Don't Tell

A good way to induce a roomful of cognitive junkies to tap into their creative reservoirs is to have them draw or sketch their ideas. This is especially valuable in Problem-Solving and new product development. However, you'll find it can also work wonders in systems and procedures upgrade sessions.

Circulate

It's important that you circulate around the room during workflow sessions. Don't stand at the front like a statue. Do the unexpected—it keeps session participants on their toes.

Don't Comment

If you comment on the quality of any idea offered by a member of the group, it has an undermining effect on productivity. By all means, feel free to ask for clarification to make sure you're boarding a person's idea accurately. And always say thank you after boarding someone's idea. That's just good process.

IDEATION EXERCISES

What follows are some Ideation exercises you can use right away in Innovation and Problem-Solving sessions. In the section following these exercises, I'll show you how to create them yourself. Remember: After you run an Ideation exercise, immediately ask the group to come up with three additional ideas or solutions pertinent to the purpose of the session. The content resulting from any Ideation exercises is irrelevant to your purpose; they are conducted simply as a means to access the creative inventory of the session participants.

Mind-Reading Exercise

Address the group as follows:

> Without conversation, please consider the consequences of everyone on the planet having the ability to read the minds of everyone else. Challenge yourselves to impose no boundaries upon the scope of your imagination. Simply list the consequences of our being able to read each other's minds. You have five minutes for this exercise. Please start.

Genie Exercise: Round 1

Ask the group to use the next five minutes to form into three teams of approximately equal size and choose one of the designated easels to use. Tell them that for this exercise they will be working together in these teams, and give them the following instruction, to be performed individually:

> Imagine that you're alone and you've just found the proverbial lamp with a genie inside. You rub the lamp, and the genie appears. The genie tells you that you have five wishes and you must decide on your list of wishes within the next four minutes. You must request exactly five wishes, not four or six. And you may not wish for an unlimited number of wishes.

177

Write your list of five wishes on a clean sheet of paper. Does anyone not understand the instruction? You have four minutes to complete this step. Please start.

Let the group know when they're within thirty seconds of the time limit. When the time is up, instruct them as follows:

Please share your list of wishes with your team. Do this orally—no need to write anything. You have five minutes. Does anyone not understand the instruction? Please start.

Again, let them know when they have thirty seconds left.

Genie Exercise: Round 2

After the group has completed the first round of the exercise, give them this directive:

The genie has changed his mind about how he wants you to handle the wishes. Now he wants each team to agree on a list of five wishes. No individual wishes will be granted unless they are among the five wishes from each team. You have ten minutes to agree on your five wishes. Select one team member to be the scribe for the group. That person's job is to help the group agree on the five team wishes and write them on the easel. The scribe can swap the role with any other person on the team after two minutes. Does anyone not understand the instruction? You have ten minutes. Please start.

Flying Exercise: Round 1

Instruct the group to take a clean sheet of paper and, without discussion, respond to the following:

Imagine how your life would change if you (and only you) could fly. You have no wings or other apparatus; you just have the ability to levitate at will and travel thousands of miles in any direction you choose at any altitude. No one knows you can do this yet.

Give them ten minutes to write down what they would do with this capability and how it would change their lives.

Flying Exercise: Round 2

As an alternative, give the group the same instruction as for Round 1, with the following twist:

Write with your left hand if you're right-handed and with your right hand if you're left-handed. If you're ambidextrous, simply alternate hands with each sentence you write. You have exactly ten minutes. Please start.

"No One Can See Me" Exercise

Address the group as follows:

> You've just discovered that you can choose to be invisible at will. Anytime you wish, you can say a secret magic phrase and become invisible for as long as you desire. Furthermore, you can pass through solids such as stone, steel, and wood. No one knows you have this secret capability. You simply have it, and you're stuck with it. What would you do with this capability in the next ten days? You have ten minutes to list the activities you'd engage in, the people you'd tell, and any changes you'd make in your life.

Swapping Exercise: Round 1

This is a good ideation alternative to keep a hardworking group from getting tired. Right after the group completes a round of Ideation, and before they share their ideas, ask them to arrange their chairs in a loose circle. If you have ten or fewer in the group, have them form a single circle. With more than ten participants, make two circles. Then give them the following instruction:

> Write your name at the top of your personal pad and pass it to the person sitting on your right. Be sure to write legibly. Then review the list you've just received from the person on your left. You may ask for clarification from the person who gave you the list, but no other discussion is permitted.

Let them know that they must write legibly for this to work properly. Each person reviews the list they've received and is allowed to ask the person next to them for clarification. No other discussion is allowed.

Give the group enough time to read the list they just received—two minutes should suffice. Ask them to raise their hands when they've finished. Use your judgment about when to move on. Some won't be ready, but don't wait for them. Speed is important here.

Now instruct the group as follows:

> Add two new ideas to the list you have in hand. You will have two minutes to do this. When I give the signal that two minutes are up, write your name on the pad next to the ideas you've added and again pass it to the person on your right.

Repeat this protocol until each person gets his or her original pad back.

This exercise can get rowdy, so be prepared. The louder the group gets, the better—that means more energy for you to work with. The group has two sources of stimuli for new ideas: the writing pads they are passing from person to person and your request for more new ideas.

Swapping Exercise: Round 2

When the first round of the Swapping Exercise has ended (all pads have returned to the original owners), move on to the second round. Keep the cycles of completion very short for this round of the exercise. Proceed with this directive to the group:

> Please stand and, without discussion, write one new idea on your pad. Don't put your name on your pad. Simply swap it with another person anywhere in the room. Then write a new idea on the pad you've just received, or build on one of the ideas already written there.

The key to this exercise is speed, and the objective is still quantity of ideas, disregarding quality. Ask the group to write as fast as they can but to write legibly. Encourage them to strive for the absurd. For this exercise, logical thought is the enemy. When you decide the time is ripe, ask them to stop. Board two ideas at a time from each participant.

Trillion Dollars Exercise: Round 1

Address the group as follows:

> You have just legitimately acquired $1 trillion. List ten things you'd do with the money in the next five days. Does anyone not understand the instruction? You have five minutes for this. Please start.

At the end of the five minutes, ask them to stop writing and request that they write three new ideas pertinent to the purpose of the session. Do not board their lists yet. Instead, proceed to the second round of this exercise.

Trillion Dollars Exercise: Round 2

Ask the group to break into teams, advising them to change team compositions (note that this is standard procedure throughout these exercises). Instruct them as follows:

> Please convene as teams, without discussion. Try to join a team with people you normally don't work with on a daily basis. You have three minutes to do this.

Once the teams are in place, give them this instruction:

> Please share with your team your list of what you'd do with $1 trillion in the next five days. Do not board your individual lists. Just share them orally for now. Does anybody not understand the instruction? You have five minutes. Please start.

At the end of the five minutes, ask each person to write three new product ideas on his or her personal pad, without discussion. Do not board these yet.

Trillion Dollars Exercise: Round 3

Now instruct the teams as follows:

> Please select a scribe for the team. The scribe's job is to board suggestions from the team. The person in this role should be changed every two minutes. As a team, achieve consensus on three things you would all agree to do with $1 trillion in the first five days.

Does anybody not understand the instruction? You have five minutes for this. Please start.

At the end of the time allotment, ask each participant to write three additional new ideas pertinent to the purpose of the session. Then take just two ideas at a time from each participant and board them.

Know-It-All Exercise: Round 1

Say to the group:

> Imagine that all of a sudden you know everything there is to know. You have no idea how this happened. What would you do in the next five days? You have five minutes to compose a list of the things you would do with all this knowledge. Does anybody not understand the instruction? Please start.

At the end of the exercise, ask the group to write three new ideas pertinent to the purpose of the session on their personal pads. Don't board these yet.

Know-It-All Exercise: Round 2

Address the group:

> Assuming you're not the one who "knows it all," what five questions would you ask a person who did know it all?

Obviously, there are multiple variations you can create for this exercise. Just don't get caught up in the content to the point where you forget to ask for three new ideas at the end of each variation.

Interconnectivity Exercise: Round 1

Instruct the group as follows:

> Without discussion, make a list of ten things, situations, or events that are not connected. Does anyone not understand the instruction? You have five minutes to complete your list. Please start.

At the end of the five minutes, ask the group to stop writing. Say to them:

> Without discussion, please identify any interconnectivity or patterns among the entries on your list. If you can't find any, what would have to change for connectivity to exist? In what way would the items on your list be connected as a result? Does anyone not understand the instruction? You have five minutes. Please start.

At the end of the five minutes, ask them to write three new ideas pertinent to the purpose of the session on their personal pads.

The Interconnectivity Exercise is even more productive when conducted as a team exercise.

Interconnectivity Exercise: Round 2

Address the group as follows:

> Without discussion, make a list of ten things that are not connected. Does anyone not understand the instruction? You have three minutes to complete your list. Please start.

At the end of the three minutes, ask the group to stop writing. Instruct them as follows:

> Please pass your pad to the person on your left. Now please identify three interconnectivities or patterns on the list you just received. You have three minutes. Please start.

At the end of the three minutes, instruct the group to stop writing and return the pads to their original owners. Then say to them:

> Without talking, write three additional new ideas pertinent to the goal of the session. Does anyone not understand the instruction? You have five minutes. Please start.

At the end of the allotted time, ask them to stop and board their ideas. Take no more than two ideas from each person and continue until you have exhausted everyone's list.

True or False Exercise

Instruct the group as follows:

> Write ten true statements not concerning yourself. You have three minutes. Please start.

At the end of the three minutes, ask the group to stop writing and give them the following directive:

> Now write ten false statements not concerning yourself. Does anyone not understand the instruction? You have three minutes. Please start.

When the time is up, give the group the following task:

> Please identify as many interconnectivities and patterns as you possibly can between the two lists and within each list. Does anybody not understand the instruction? You have five minutes. Please start.

At the end of the five minutes, ask the group to stop and direct them to write five new ideas related to the purpose of the workflow session. Take no more than one new idea from each person at a time and board them.

Big Question Exercise

Say to the group:

> Without discussion, please write your answer to this question: "What's the biggest question you can think

of?" Does anybody not understand the instruction? You have two minutes. Please start.

At the end of the allotted time, instruct the group as follows:

You have one minute to ask a bigger question. Please start.

Repeat the process for at least three rounds. Then, without pausing, say to the group:

Please write three new ideas pertinent to the purpose of this workflow session. You have three minutes. Please start.

Small Question Exercise

Follow up the preceding Big Question Exercise with these instructions:

Without discussion, please write your answer to the following question: "What's the smallest question you can think of?"Does anybody not understand the instruction? You have two minutes. Please start.

At the end of the allotted time, instruct the group as follows:

You have one minute to ask an even smaller question. Please start.

Repeat the process for at least two rounds. Then, without pausing, say:

> Please write three new ideas pertinent to the purpose of this workflow session. You have three minutes. Please start.

Note: In addition to serving as Ideation vehicles, the Big Question and Small Question exercises enable participants to upgrade their ability to expand and contract operating context at will. For example, some issues or problems are so complex that they are easier to resolve by reducing (or reframing) them into several smaller questions. Similarly, the ability to identify patterns and interconnectivities among problems reveals systemic solutions. This ability to consciously reframe issues, situations, problems, and opportunities is a priceless workflow management skill.

Ask the Group

As a change of pace in an Ideation phase that's well under way and productive, address the group as follows:

> Imagine you're the facilitator of this workflow session. Create one new Ideation exercise that you think would be worth conducting with this group. Does anyone not understand the instruction? You have three minutes. Please start.

At the end of the three minutes, take one Ideation exercise from each person and board it. When all suggestions have been displayed, assign a number to each suggestion and address the group as follows:

> Please review all of the Ideation exercises and decide on the one that you'd most like to conduct. Please write your choices on your pads. Are there any questions? You have five minutes. Please start.

At the end of the allotted time, ask for each person's choice and place a check mark next to that exercise on the boarded list. The exercise with the largest number of check marks is the group choice.

Now run that exercise. Don't forget to ask for three new ideas from each person upon its completion. Also, be sure to thank the author of the exercise that was selected.

If the yield from that exercise was good, consider a repeat. You may also choose to run the next most popular exercise in the same manner. Continue with the group's exercises as long as the process is producing new ideas and the group is enthused.

Pairs Exercise

Everyone is different, and some people find it easier to be creative in a one-on-one situation. To take advantage of this in a group Ideation setting, address the group as follows:

> Please pair off with another person—someone with whom you have minimal contact on a daily basis.

Bring your writing pad and pen. Position your chairs so that you're facing each other. Spread out to isolate yourselves from the other pairs as much as possible.

Once the group is arranged in pairs, instruct them as follows:

Please write down just one new idea relevant to the purpose of the session. Be sure to write legibly. Any questions? You have one minute for this. Please start.

At the end of the minute, instruct the group as follows:

Please exchange writing pads and read your partner's idea. Now add just one other idea right below it. Again, please write legibly. You have one minute for this. Please start.

When the minute is up, repeat the cycle once again. Repeat this for at least three cycles or until you sense the productivity level is waning. Then board each pair's ideas. Request that they remain with their partners. Then address the pairs as follows:

Please set aside one of your writing pads and one person from each pair respond to the following: "What question needs to be asked now?" Please write your question on the pad without talking and pass the pad to your partner to read. If you're the one receiving the pad, read your partner's question and write a better or bigger question on the pad. Then return the pad for your partner to do likewise. Exchange pads at least three times.

After they've completed the third cycle, instruct the pairs as follows:

Now, instead of writing questions, write new ideas (or solutions). Pass the pad back and forth until each of you has written at least three new ideas or solutions pertinent to the purpose of the session. Feel free to build on each other's thoughts. When you've finished, relax until everyone else has finished.

When you see that everyone has finished, ask the pairs to share their new ideas, and board them.

SWITCH SESSIONS

If you find yourself with a stalled Problem-Solving Session, you can rejuvenate the group by switching gears to an Innovation Session mode and running an Ideation exercise. This immediately recharges the dynamics in the conference room. New energy is injected, and status quo thinking is replaced by creative speculation unrelated to the task of solving the problem at hand.

When you decide to use this option, remember to utilize the time gap right after the Ideation exercise to solicit additional

---

solutions from the group. Then return to the Problem-Solving mode. As a general rule, whenever you complete an Ideation exercise, immediately ask the group to write three additional new ideas. (I know I'm repeating myself on this issue, but you'll understand why I'm doing it when you run your first Innovation Session.)

Be assured that the window of innovative opportunity is normally quite short before individuals relapse into habitual thinking patterns. One of your primary responsibilities as a facilitator is to create an environment that makes it easy for people to break out of their habitual thinking patterns at will.

HOW TO DO IT YOURSELF

Notice that almost all of the Ideation exercises you've read about here are expansive in nature—all of them allude to *options* the participants don't have. Options are the secret for developing Ideation exercises. Everyone wants more options. That's why so many people want more money and more power; it gives them more options.

If you want to expand the operating context of a group, get them to fantasize for a few minutes about an option they don't have. This gets them outside their normal thinking mode or comfort zone and gives you a window of opportunity through which to ask them for novel ideas and solutions. But you have to act quickly because the window shuts pretty fast.

However, you now know how to open it again and again—which means you have access to an unlimited inventory of creative exercises to access the innovative potential of yourself and others again and again. That skill makes you even more valuable to your organization.

FINAL THOUGHTS

Given the nature of our technology-driven global economy, all organizations and institutions must be innovative entities to remain relevant, let alone competitive. While it's no secret that the speed with which technology is evolving is not matched by the human factor, I believe that every organization already employs the intellectual and creative talent it needs to be successful. The fly in the ointment is the fact that few managers know how to leverage the intellectual and creative resources of the individuals who report to them. In previous chapters, we've provided the means for managers to correct this situation with three workflow management sessions that elevate collaboration to the digital age standard.

The fourth workflow management component, Ongoing Planning, provides a means to capitalize on the interconnectivities created by technology's warp-speed evolution. Significantly, it reframes the planning function from a scheduled event carried out by a few to an ongoing process involving many.

The collaborative sessions are interrelated and designed to be introduced in a particular sequence: Issues Management first, followed by Innovation, and then Problem-Solving. The Ongoing Planning Database cannot be installed until the three collaborative sessions are in place.

A management team can choose to adopt the Issues Management process only and not add the others. That alone has a transformative effect on the workflow management practices and collaborative outcomes in any organization.

Adoption of the Innovation process can be delayed until meetings have been replaced by Issues Management Sessions. Adding the Innovation process later enables an organization to develop top-tier innovative capabilities within a very short time span.

The Problem-Solving Session, as you know, utilizes elements of both the Issues Management and the Innovation sessions. The structure and guiding principles of the sessions enable managers to upgrade the quality of thought utilized to manage issues, solve problems, and recognize opportunities. Unquestionably, nothing is more critical to an organization's success than the quality of its intellectual and creative capital, which, when properly applied, becomes intellectual and creative equity.

In conclusion, the collaborative sessions empower managers to leverage human capital and develop innovation and speed-to-market capabilities—vital competencies for success in the digital age. Ongoing Planning, the fourth part of the equation, enables the creation of sustainable value.

Appendix 1

GROUP SESSION GUIDES

ISSUES MANAGEMENT SESSION

PURPOSE: Discuss and verify the purpose of the session, for example, to identify, resolve, and allocate for resolution all Critical Issues.

- Explain your role as facilitator.

AGREEMENT: Establish the agreement.

DIFFERENCES: Explain the difference between meetings and workflow management sessions.

CONTENT AND PROCESS: Explain the terms *content* and *process*.

INFORMATION GAPS: Explain the nature and role of Information Gaps.

SPEED: Explain the role of speed in all workflow management sessions.

NO DISCUSSION: Explain the reason for a "no discussion" instruction.

- Confirm that everyone in the group understands your instructions before you instruct them to start any task.

ISSUES: Define and discuss the Issues.

- Instruct the group to write "Issues" on their notepads.
- Collect and display everyone's list of issues.

CRITICAL ISSUES: Identify the Critical Issues.

BOARD: Display the Critical Issues on the board at the front of the group.

NUMBER: Number all Critical Issues, for ease of identification.

RANK: Rank all Critical Issues.

- Identify the top five Critical Issues.

QUESTION EXERCISE: Run the Question Exercise.

- Collect and board the first round of Questions.
- Ask for a better question.
- Collect and board the second round of Questions.
- Are there any additions to or deletions from the list of issues?

RESOLVE: Ask the group if the first issue can be resolved immediately.

- If yes: Resolve the first issue.
- Promote the resolved issue to the Action Plan.
- If no: Decide on the Next Steps for resolving the issue (i.e., via Problem-Solving Session, Innovation Session, reallocation, postponement, or other means) and promote it to the Action Plan.
- Ask the group if the second issue can be resolved, and repeat the process until all Critical Issues have been addressed.

ACTION PLAN: Complete the Action Plan components: Tasks, Responsibilities, Report, and Due Date.

END SESSION.

INNOVATION SESSION

PURPOSE: Discuss and agree on the purpose of the session, for example, to develop new product concepts.

- Explain your role as the facilitator.

AGREEMENT: Establish the agreement.

DIFFERENCES: Explain the difference between conventional meetings and workflow management sessions.

CONTENT AND PROCESS: Explain the terms *content* and *process.*

INFORMATION GAPS: Explain the nature and role of Information Gaps.

SPEED: Explain the role of speed in all workflow management sessions.

DISCUSSION: Explain the reason for a "no discussion" instruction.

- Confirm that everyone in the group understands your instructions before you tell them to start any task.

- Identify and explain the four Innovation Session phases: Ideation, Building, Evaluation, and Action Plan.

- Explain why it's important to keep the Ideation and Building phases separate from the Evaluation phase.

LOGISTICS: Let the group know about session length and breaks, and that it's okay for anyone to leave the session at any time. Ask them to set their cell phones to vibrate and take any calls outside the conference room.

CHANGE: Ask participants to sit in different seats after each break.

TOP OF MIND: Instruct the group to write the heading "Ideas" on their pads (and you do the same on your easel). Instruct them to get all ideas onto paper as quickly as possible (three-minute time limit).

DISPLAY: Go around the room and request that each participant read aloud one or two ideas. Resist the urge to take more than two issues at a time, especially with a large group. Display the ideas.

IDEATION: Ask the group to use the ideas on the wall to trigger additional new product ideas (three-minute time limit). Explain the importance of suspending judgment during this phase of the session. Urge them to go for quantity of issues and to embrace absurdity.

DISPLAY: Take just one or two ideas from each person and board them. Decide if you want to go for a third Ideation round.

IDEATION: If so, ask them to use the ideas of others in the group to trigger one additional new product idea (three-minute time limit).

DISPLAY: Take just one idea from each person at a time and board them.

BREAKS: When it's time for a break, instruct participants to sit in different seats when they return.

QUESTION EXERCISE: Explain the purpose and ensure that everyone in the group has a clear understanding of its role in the Problem-Solving process. Give them three minutes to come up with three questions.

IDEATION: Instruct the group to write at least three new ideas within three minutes.

BETTER QUESTION: Challenge the group to ask a better question and define what you mean by this (two-minute time limit).

IDEATION: Instruct the group to write at least three new ideas (three-minute time limit).

MIND-READING EXERCISE: Run this exercise for ten minutes.

SHARE: Let the participants share their lists, but do not display them.

IDEATION: As they listen to the mind-reading lists of others, give them three minutes to come up with three new ideas.

DISPLAY: Accept two new ideas from each person per round, and board them.

IDEATION: Instruct the group to write at least two new ideas per person (three-minute time limit).

DISPLAY: Accept one new idea from each person per round, and board them.

BREAK: Allow ten minutes. Ask participants to change seats upon their return.

GENIE EXERCISE 1: Have participants break into teams and write individual wish lists, with no discussion (ten-minute time limit).

GENIE EXERCISE 2: Have participants break into teams and produce a team wish list, with discussion (ten-minute time limit).

IDEATION: Allow the group three minutes to come up with three new ideas per person. Display them on your easel.

DISPLAY: Team scribes mount the team wish lists at the front of the room.

IDEATION: Give the group three minutes to come up with three new ideas per person.

GROUP WISH LIST: Challenge the group to agree on a group wish list of only five wishes. Allow five minutes, with group discussion. You function as scribe for the group. Display the wish list on your easel.

IDEATION: Allow the group three minutes to come up with three new ideas. Monitor the group's energy level.

QUESTION EXERCISE: Do not display questions.

IDEATION: Give the group two minutes to come up with two new ideas per question.

Building

SWITCH TO BUILDING PHASE: Inform the group that they're now switching to the Building phase of the Innovation Session. Take a ten-minute break, if appropriate.

CHANGE TEAMS: Again break the group into teams with a different composition.

EXPLAIN: Explain the Building process.

TEAM DISPLAYS: Reconvene as a group. Team representatives display the outcomes at the front of the room.

IDEATION: Allow the group three minutes to come up with two new ideas per person.

DISPLAY: Accept one new idea per person per round. Board the new ideas as they're shared.

Evaluation

SWITCH TO EVALUATION PHASE: Inform the group that they're now switching to the Evaluation phase and explain this process.

CONCEPT-BUILDING: Explain how to convert new product ideas to concepts.

IDEATION: Identify new ideas, concepts, combinations, patterns, interconnectivities, etc. (five-minute time limit).

DISPLAY: Record all of the preceding.

CONCEPT-RANKING: Explain the ranking protocol to the group and implement it.

ACTION PLAN: Tasks/Next Steps; Responsibilities; Report; Due Date (Information Gaps are included under Tasks/Next Steps).

END SESSION.

PROBLEM-SOLVING SESSION

ROLE: Explain your role as the facilitator.

PURPOSE: Discuss and agree on the purpose of the session.

AGREEMENT: Establish the agreement.

- Explain the difference between conventional meetings and workflow management sessions.

- Explain your role as facilitator.

CONTENT AND PROCESS: Explain the terms *content* and *process*.

SPEED: Explain the role of speed in all workflow management sessions.

DISCUSSION: Explain the reason for a "no discussion" instruction.

INSTRUCTIONS: Confirm that everyone in the group understands your instructions before you tell them to start any task.

LOGISTICS: Let the group know about session length and breaks and that it's okay for anyone to leave the session at any time between the scheduled breaks. Tell them to set cell phones to vibrate and take any calls outside the conference room.

- Instruct participants to sit in different seats after each break.

INFORMATION GAPS: Position an easel at the front of the conference room. Explain its use in the Problem-Solving process.

PATTERNS/INTERCONNECTIVITIES: Board all problems on separate sheets and instruct the group to write down any patterns or interconnectivities they observe (three-minute time limit).

DISPLAY: Accept and board just one observation from each person per round.

NO EVALUATION: Remind the group that there can be no evaluation during the Ideation stage of the Problem-Solving Session.

VERIFY: Verify the problem by conducting a What-If Exercise (five-minute time limit).

CONSENSUS: Agree on the definition of the problem.

SOLUTIONS: Ask the group to write three possible solutions to the problem being addressed (five-minute time limit).

DISPLAY: Accept one suggested solution from each person per round.

SOLUTION FOUND?: Determine whether there is consensus that a particular solution or a combination of solutions has been found.

- If yes: Proceed to the Action Plan and include Information Gaps.

ENTRY POINTS: Explain what these are and their role.

QUESTION EXERCISE: Run a Question Exercise (three-minute time limit).

DISPLAY: Accept just one question per person per round and board them.

BETTER QUESTION: Without pause or comment, instruct the group to ask a better question.

SOLUTION: Ask whether anyone thinks a solution has been found or is close to being found. Allow group discussion for this (five-minute time limit).

- If yes: Proceed to the Action Plan and include the Information Gaps.

- If no: Proceed to Solution-Building.

Solution-Building

SOLUTION-BUILDING: Instruct the group to break into teams of four to six individuals each. Ask the group to identify a solution to the problem, building on each other's ideas and not censoring their imaginations (ten-minute time limit).

CONVERGE: Instruct the teams to return to the group format. Request one representative of each group to display their solutions or partial solutions. Invite the group to collectively determine whether a solution has been found or if some combination of solutions can be integrated to constitute a viable solution. Allow unrestricted communication (your discretion regarding time allotment).

HARVEST: This is the critical-path event in the Problem-Solving Session. People will be talking at the same time. Find a balance between chaos and structure. Write fast. Stay out of the fray, but be ready to resume command if things get out of control; the mother lode can usually be found at this intersection of chaos and structure.

SOLUTION FOUND: Proceed to the Action Plan and address the next problem, if appropriate.

WHEN TO STOP: Two of the most common reasons for not resolving a problem are group fatigue and time constraints. If your group is having trouble identifying the solution to a problem at this point in the session, they need an Ideation exercise to stimulate their creativity.

IDEATION EXERCISE: Run a quick Ideation exercise and return to the Problem-Solving Session.

END SESSION: When a solution has been found, proceed to the Action Plan and end the session.

Appendix 2

ONE-ON-ONE SESSION GUIDES

ONE-ON-ONE ISSUES MANAGEMENT SESSION

PURPOSE: Discuss and verify the purpose of the session (to identify, resolve, and/or allocate issues for resolution).

YOUR ROLE: Explain your role as facilitator.

AGREEMENT: Establish the agreement.

- Explain the difference between meetings and workflow management sessions.

CONTENT AND PROCESS: Explain the terms *content* and *process*.

INFORMATION GAPS: Explain the nature and role of Information Gaps.

SPEED: Explain the role of speed in all workflow management sessions.

ISSUES: Define and discuss *issues*.

- Instruct your associate to write "Issues" on his or her notepad.

- Collect and display these issues.

CRITICAL ISSUES: Identify Critical Issues.

BOARD: Board the Critical Issues.

NUMBER: Number all Critical Issues for ease of identification.

RANK: Rank the Critical Issues.

- Identify the top five Critical Issues.

QUESTION EXERCISE: Run the Question Exercise.

- Collect and board the first round of questions.

- Ask for a better question.

- Run the second round of the Question Exercise.

- Collect and board the second round of questions.

- Determine whether there are any additions to or deletions from the list of issues.

- Ask whether the first issue can be resolved immediately.

- If yes: Resolve it and promote it to the Action Plan.

END SESSION, or resolve the next issue.

- If no: Determine the Next Steps for resolving the issue (via a Problem-Solving Session, Innovation Session, reallocation, postponement, or other means) and promote it to the Action Plan.

- Repeat the process until all Critical Issues have been addressed.

ACTION PLAN: Complete the Action Plan components.

END SESSION. (Switching roles during a one-on-one Issues Management Session would be done for training purposes only.)

ONE-ON-ONE INNOVATION SESSION

PURPOSE: Discuss and verify the purpose of the session (e.g., "to discover preemptive brand-positioning opportunities").

YOUR ROLE: Explain your role as facilitator.

AGREEMENT: Establish the agreement.

- Explain the difference between conventional meetings and workflow management sessions.

CONTENT AND PROCESS: Explain the terms *content* and *process.*

INFORMATION GAPS: Explain the nature and role of Information Gaps.

SPEED: Explain the role of speed in all workflow management sessions.

INNOVATION SESSION PHASES: Explain to your associate that all Innovation Sessions are composed of four phases: *Ideation, Building, Evaluation,* and *Action Plan.*

STARTING: After a brief discussion with your partner, write up your understanding of the session goal.

INFORMATION GAPS: Write "Information Gaps" on your easel.

TOP OF MIND: Instruct your associate to write down any ideas he or she already has about new brand-positioning opportunities (three-minute time limit).

DISPLAY: At the end of the allotted time, display your colleague's ideas on your easel.

QUESTION EXERCISE: Explain the purpose of this exercise, and request that your associate write as many questions as possible in the next three minutes.

- Do not board your associate's questions yet. Instead, instruct your associate to ask a better question (three-minute time limit).

IDEATION: Ask your associate to write as many new brand-positioning ideas as possible within the next three minutes.

DISPLAY: Board the outcome of the preceding step.

MIND-READING EXERCISE: Run the Mind-Reading Exercise with your associate (maximum five-minute time limit).

SHARE: Ask your associate to share his or her list with you, but do not board the results.

IDEATION: Instruct your associate to write at least three more new positioning ideas (three-minute time limit).

DISPLAY: Board the outcome of the preceding step.

GENIE EXERCISE: Run the Genie Exercise for your associate (five-minute time limit).

SHARE: Ask your colleague to share his or her list, but do not board the results.

IDEATION: Request that your partner write at least three more new positioning ideas (three-minute time limit).

DISPLAY: Board your associate's new ideas.

BUILDING PHASE: Let your associate know that you're now switching to the Building phase of the one-on-one Innovation Session. Explain the Building phase within the context of a group session vs. a one-on-one session. Explain how the Building phase is utilized in a group setting, and guide your associate to customize the process for a one-on-one format.

IDEATION: Ask your associate what new positioning ideas have arisen as a consequence of the building process (three-minute time limit).

DISPLAY: Board the outcome of the preceding step.

EVALUATION PHASE: Let your associate know that you're now switching to the Evaluation phase of the one-on-one Innovation Session.

CONCEPT-BUILDING: Explain how to convert new product (or positioning) ideas to concepts.

IDEATION: Identify new ideas, concepts, combinations, patterns, interconnectivities, etc. (five-minute time limit).

DISPLAY: Board the outcome from the preceding step.

CONCEPT-RANKING: Explain the ranking process and implement it.

SWITCH ROLES: If your partner is capable of facilitating a one-on-one Innovation Session, switch roles and run the session again with you as the participant.

ACTION PLAN: Promote the most viable concepts to Action Plan status. Include all Information Gaps. Switch roles if your partner knows how to run a one-on-one Innovation Session.

ONE-ON-ONE PROBLEM-SOLVING SESSION

PURPOSE: Discuss and verify the purpose of the session (e.g., "how do we curb the high turnover of senior sales personnel and the resultant loss of their accounts?").

FACILITATOR: Explain your role as facilitator.

AGREEMENT: Establish the agreement.

- Explain the difference between conventional meetings and workflow management sessions.

CONTENT AND PROCESS: Explain the terms *content* and *process.*

INFORMATION GAPS: Explain the nature and role of Information Gaps.

SPEED: Explain the role of speed in all workflow management sessions.

PATTERNS/INTERCONNECTIVITIES: Board all problems on a separate sheet and instruct your colleague to write down any patterns or interconnectivities he or she observes (three-minute time limit).

DISPLAY: Board all observations from the preceding step.

NO EVALUATION: Remind your associate that there can be no evaluating or judging during the Ideation stages of the one-on-one Problem-Solving Session.

VERIFY PROBLEM: Run a What-If Exercise (five-minute time limit).

SOLUTIONS: Instruct your associate to write at least three possible solutions within five minutes.

DISPLAY: Board the solutions and partial solutions.

SOLUTION FOUND: Ask your associate if he or she believes a solution has been found.

- If yes: Proceed to the Action Plan. Include all Information Gaps.

END SESSION.

- If no: Continue with the Problem-Solving Session (or change roles, if your associate knows how to run a one-on-one Problem-Solving Session).

ENTRY POINTS, LEVERAGE, AND QUESTIONS: Explain the role of each in the Problem-Solving Session.

QUESTION EXERCISE: Run a Question Exercise (three-minute time limit).

DISPLAY: Board the questions.

BETTER QUESTION: Without pause or comment, instruct your colleague to ask a better question.

SOLUTION FOUND: If a solution has been found, proceed to the Action Plan. Include all Information Gaps.

END SESSION OR SWITCH ROLES.

IDEATION: If a solution has not been found, run the Mind-Reading Exercise (five-minute time limit).

SOLUTIONS: Without pause, ask your associate to write three possible solutions to the problem (three-minute time limit).

DISPLAY: Board the suggested solutions.

SOLUTION FOUND: Ask your associate if he or she believes a solution has been found.

- If yes: Proceed to the Action Plan. Include all Information Gaps.

- If no: Change roles.

OR: Schedule the problem for a group Problem-Solving Session.

Appendix 3

SOLO SESSION GUIDES

SOLO ISSUES MANAGEMENT SESSION

ISSUES: Create a file labeled "Issues."

- List all the issues. Don't prioritize them.

CRITICAL ISSUES: Identify with an asterisk any issue you consider critical.

RANK: Rank the issues in the order in which you need to get them resolved.

RESOLUTION STATUS: Determine whether you can resolve it yourself now.

- If "yes": Do so.

- If "no": (1) Delegate it, or (2) schedule it for a group Issues Management Session.

RESOLUTION STATUS: Dispose of all issues you don't intend to resolve immediately in this manner.

RESIST: Do not resort to a to-do list. Use your Personal Workflow Planner instead.

WORKFLOW PLANNER: Enter the Next Steps in your Workflow Planner.

SOLO INNOVATION SESSION

PURPOSE: For example, "identify business development strategies."

BRIDGING: You'll be running this session without the benefit of a facilitator.

SESSION PHASES: Implement the session phases: *Ideation, Building, Evaluation,* and *Action Plan.*

DON'T MIX: Keep the Ideation and Building phases separate from Evaluation.

SPEED: Just because you're alone in this session doesn't mean speed doesn't count.

INFORMATION GAPS: All Information Gaps are potential gold mines—including those you discover in solo sessions.

PURPOSE: In solo Innovation, you need to be as clear about what you're looking for as you would with a roomful of others. Always be looking for the next billion-dollar idea for your organization.

EMPTY MIND: You already have lots of ideas on the subject. The first step is to get all of those ideas down so you can start the process with an empty mind.

QUESTION EXERCISE: Give yourself three minutes for the Question Exercise.

BETTER QUESTION: Without pause, challenge yourself to come up with a better question (three-minute time limit).

IDEATION: Challenge yourself to come up with five new business ideas within the next five minutes. Don't evaluate!

- Run the "No One Can See Me" Ideation exercise.

DISPLAY: Review your output from the preceding exercise for stimuli.

IDEATE: Without pause, write as many new business ideas as you can within the next five minutes. Don't evaluate any of these.

SKETCH OPTION: Without pause, take a large sheet of paper and sketch two additional ideas. Don't use words; just do what you can with symbols or squiggly lines or crazy circles (or whatever) to communicate an additional idea, or two, or three. No one is going to see this stuff. Just do it. (Three-minute time limit.)

IDEATE: At the end of the time limit, write three new ideas.

IDEATE: Select another Ideation exercise from the list in Chapter 8, "Making It Happen," and perform it yourself. Write three new ideas.

BUILD: The key to successful Building is to focus on why something could work as opposed to why it probably won't. Look at all of your ideas, partial ideas, patterns, interconnectivities, and possible combinations.

- Record all of the new business ideas you uncover by building, combining, merging, connecting, and bridging.

Evaluation

EVALUATE: Review each idea or concept and assign it a viability value ranging from 1 to 3, with 1 being the best. These are new business concepts that you'll want to share with others.

WORKFLOW PLANNER: Enter the Next Steps in your Workflow Planner.

END SESSION.

SOLO PROBLEM-SOLVING SESSION

PURPOSE: State the problem to be solved.

INFORMATION GAPS: Create a file labeled "Information Gaps" in which to record questions that occur to you but for which you do not have the answers.

ENTRY POINT: Select the best Entry Point to resolve the problem.

QUESTION EXERCISE: Run this exercise at least twice to verify your understanding of the problem.

RESTATE PROBLEM: Do this only if necessary.

PATTERN RECOGNITION: Determine whether the answer to the problem has been suggested.

- If "yes": Enter it in your Workflow Planner.

END SESSION.

RESTATE PROBLEM: If necessary, restate the problem and repeat the solo Problem-Solving Session.

REFRAME: Run a What-If Exercise and see whether an answer to the problem is suggested.

- If "yes": Make an entry in your Workflow Planner and end the session.

- If "no": Continue the session.

IDEATION: Run an Ideation exercise.

SOLUTION: Determine whether an answer to the problem has been suggested.

- If "yes": Make an entry in your Workflow Planner.

- If "no": Consider scheduling the problem for inclusion in the next group Problem-Solving Session. Make an entry in your Workflow Planner.

END SESSION.

INDEX

223